Herbert Puchta, Jeff Stranks and Peter

English in Mind

* Student's Book 5

CAMBRIDGE
UNIVERSITY PRESS

Listening	Speaking	Reading	Writing
Different animal abilities	Talking about 'sixth sense' in animals and people	Animals know before Literature: *Call of the Wild*	Animal story
A book review programme	Interviews Pronunciation: sounding polite or angry	Listening with your eyes	Letter of complaint
Careers talk about advertising	Designing and presenting a marketing campaign for a product of your choice	Advertising: the logic of emotions Culture: The Ultimate Refund	Covering letter of application
Radio programme on how to cope with stress Song: *Stand My Ground*	Talking about your reactions in stressful situations	Fight or flight? Dealing with stress	Report and proposal
Two women spies	Talking about crime movies Giving a short talk based on a picture	Behind the scenes – true stories from the movies Literature: *Charlotte Gray*	A biography
Phone-in / game show: *A Likely Story*	A story or anecdote Pronunciation: stress in phrases	The rise and rise of urban legends	Newspaper article
An interview about metaphors	Discussing what inspires your own creativity	What inspires the inspirational? Culture: Inspired Buildings	Poem with metaphors and similes
Virtual holidays Song: *Virtual World*	Talking about virtual holidays	The Entropia Universe	Informal letter or email turning down an invitation
Mirroring techniques	Talking about learning through imitation	A revealing reflection Literature: *Life of Pi*	Discursive composition
Conversation about cheating in sport	Talking about sports events and athletes Short monologues Pronunciation: linking sounds	Sport in the news	Description of a sporting event (magazine)
Candidates audition for a reality TV show	Talking about superheroes Designing and presenting a group of superheroes	Superheroes – Have you got what it takes? Culture: Superheroes around the world	Film review
Teenagers talk about being on their own Song: *Message in a Bottle*	Discussing what it would be like to live completely on your own Talking about what to take to a desert island	Island diary	A leaflet
People of different ages comment on the reading text	Talking about life choices	The Battle of the Generations Literature: Two poems about ageing: *Beautiful Old Age* and *A Madrigal*	Formal letter to a magazine editor
A scientist: extending life expectancy	Conversations / discussions Pronunciation: stress and intonation	Hard talk – cosmetic surgery	Report and article
Suggesting items for the museum	Discussing objects for a People's Museum Taking part in a discussion to plan a school trip	The People's Museum Culture: Museums around the world	A note
Radio film review of *Freaky Friday* Song: *My Generation*	Discussing 'swapping places' in a family	Culture Shock	Meaningless proverbs and cinquains

Module 1
Logic and intuition

YOU WILL LEARN ABOUT ...

- Amazing animal behaviour ....
- Interview language ....
- Women in music ....
- Shopping behaviour ....
- Advertising ....
- How humans behave in fight or flight situations ....

- ✳ Can you match each picture with a topic?

YOU WILL LEARN HOW TO ...

Speak
- Talk about the 'sixth sense' in animals and people
- Talk about equal rights for men and women
- Hold an interview with someone
- Talk about your reactions in stressful situations
- Design and present a marketing campaign for a product of your choice

Write
- An animal story
- A letter of complaint
- A covering letter of application
- A report and proposal

Read
- An article about animals that sense natural disasters long before humans do
- An article about a woman who successfully fought for her rights
- A magazine article about what makes us buy what we buy
- A magazine article explaining what 'fight or flight' is

Listen
- A radio quiz about the amazing world of animals
- A radio review about a book called *Blink*
- A web advertising expert talking about his job
- A radio programme on how to cope with stress

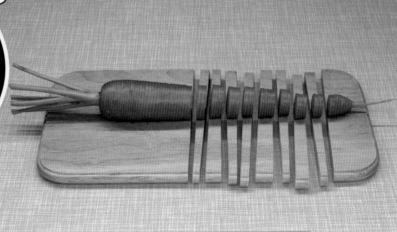

Use grammar

Can you match the names of the grammar points with the examples?

Past perfect continuous	This time she knew she **would** win.
Past perfect passive	In stressful situations my mind **tends to** go blank.
Future in the past	**Surprisingly**, the answer was yes.
Adjective order	If the city **had not been evacuated**, a lot of people **would have been killed**.
Position of adverbs	The night before the tsunami hit, the elephants **had been making** strange noises.
Talking about tendencies	She's got a **gorgeous dark brown** Italian Jacket.

Use vocabulary

Can you think of two more examples for each topic?

Animal sounds	Making decisions	Advertising	Coping with stress
hiss	jump to a conclusion	commercial	take a break
bark	a snap decision	slogan	put your feet up
....	....	....	....
....	....	....	....

1 Animal instincts

* Past perfect tenses review
* Vocabulary: animal sounds

1 Read and listen

(a) Work with a partner. Make a list of the characteristics and abilities elephants have.

(b) 🔊 Read and listen to the text. Choose a title 1–4 that you think fits best and say why.

1 Lucky escapes
2 Nature's advanced warning systems
3 How elephants help humans
4 Scientific uncertainty about animals

Animals know before

The elephant is Thailand's most revered animal. Elephants are respected for their supposed wisdom, strength and good fortune. Over the centuries, they have also been credited with being able to sense earthquakes, storms and other disasters long before humans do. The behaviour of elephants before and during the 2004 South Asia earthquake and tsunami has added to this reputation. After the tsunami, reports circulated around Thailand that elephants had performed miraculous feats when the waves hit, snatching people up out of the fast-rising water with their trunks and pulling them out of harm's way.

An elephant handler in Khao Lak, one of the worst hit areas on Thailand's southwestern coast, said: 'On the night before the tsunami hit, the elephants had been making strange noises. I had never heard them scream like that before, so I ran out to the house where they were sleeping because I thought that there was something wrong with them. A group of people working at a nearby rubber plant were also really frightened by the elephants' screams, and they begged me to calm them down.' Five minutes before the tsunami hit the coast, the elephants, standing in chains waiting to take tourists on treks, began screaming again. One of them broke free and ran uphill. Another one carrying tourists on its back also bolted to safety.

It is thought that elephants have a sixth sense that shouldn't be ignored. Some scientists think that elephants can tune in to the low-frequency vibrations that precede a tsunami or earthquake. And it is not just elephants. At Yala National Park in Sri Lanka, for example, few animals of any kind appear to have died in the tsunami, although tens of thousands of people lost their lives there.

This is not, of course, a new idea. It has been thought for centuries that animals can predict earthquakes, and there is plenty of evidence to base this belief on. As far back as 373 BC, the Greek city of Helices was destroyed by an earthquake, but in the days leading up to it, the city had been abandoned by most of its animals. More recently, an earthquake struck California in 1994 and killed 57 people. Police said that many pets had been reported missing in the previous week. And not only earthquakes: in 2004, scientists in Florida noted that electronically tagged sharks had been behaving strangely during the approach of a hurricane.

But precisely what these animals sensed remains a mystery. One theory is that they felt the Earth vibrate before humans did. Other ideas suggest they detected gases that had been released from the Earth or electric charges in the air.

One of the world's most earthquake-prone countries is Japan,

where devastation has taken countless lives and caused enormous damage to property. Researchers in Japan have long studied animals in the hope of discovering what they hear or feel before the Earth shakes, and then using that sense as a prediction tool.

American seismologists, on the other hand, are sceptical. A recent report by the experts on earthquakes, the United States Geological Survey (USGS) said that a connection between erratic animal behaviour and the occurrence of an earthquake has never been scientifically established. The USGS carried out tests into animal predictions in the 1970s but no further investigations into the theory have been carried out since. 'What we're faced with is a lot of anecdotes,' says Andy Michael, a geophysicist at USGS. 'Animals react to so many things: being hungry, defending their territories, predators, and so on. So it's often hard to know if their behaviour is an advanced warning signal or something else.'

Rupert Sheldrake, a biologist and expert on canine behaviour, disagrees. Sheldrake studied animal reactions before major tremors, including the earthquake in Northridge, California, in 1994, and the Greek and Turkish earthquakes in 1999. 'Similar patterns of peculiar animal behaviour before an earthquake strikes have been reported independently by people all

c Read the text again. Mark the statements *T* (true) or *F* (false). Correct the false statements.

1 Elephants are highly respected animals in Thailand. `T`

2 In the 2004 tsunami, elephants saved some people. ☐

3 Some scientists think that elephants can hear an earthquake starting. ☐

4 Animals can only sense the approach of tsunamis or earthquakes. ☐

5 For some time, Japanese scientists have been studying how animals sense danger. ☐

6 Scientists at the USGS think it's hard to know what causes certain animal behaviour. ☐

7 Rupert Sheldrake believes that there is a connection between strange animal behaviour and earthquakes. ☐

8 More than 150,000 people died in the Haicheng earthquake. ☐

d Find the words 1–9 in the text and match each one to a definition a–i.

1 revered (paragraph 1)
2 out of harm's way (paragraph 1)
3 worst hit (paragraph 2)
4 broke free (paragraph 2)
5 bolted to safety (paragraph 2)
6 the days leading up to (paragraph 4)
7 countless (paragraph 6)
8 erratic (paragraph 7)
9 link (paragraph 8)

a ran very quickly to a safe place
b most badly damaged
c the time immediately before
d escaped
e greatly respected
f connection
g a very large number of
h to a safe place
i always changing

Discussion box

Work in pairs or small groups. Discuss these questions together.

1 The text mentions a sixth sense. What is this sixth sense, and what are the other five?

2 Do you believe that animals or humans have a sixth sense? If yes, give examples to support your belief.

3 What kind of situations do you think that humans would use a sixth sense in?

over the world. I cannot believe that there's no link,' he says. 'Just think of the earthquake in Haicheng in China in 1975. Chinese officials ordered the population of one million to evacuate the city after numerous incidents of erratic animal behaviour had been observed: for example, snakes crawling out of holes in the ground. Only a small portion of the population was hurt or killed. If the city had not been evacuated, it is estimated that the number of fatalities and injuries could have exceeded 150,000.'

Perhaps this sixth sense that some animals appear to have can help us in the future to protect ourselves from natural disaster or, at least, to minimise the effects.

2 Grammar

Past perfect continuous, past perfect simple and past perfect passive review

a Look at the examples from the text. Which one is an example of: the past perfect continuous, the past perfect simple or the past perfect passive?

1 *Other ideas suggest they detected gases that had been released from the Earth.*

2 *On the night before the tsunami hit, the elephants had been making strange noises.*

3 *After the tsunami, reports circulated around Thailand that elephants had performed miraculous feats.*

b Read the text again. Find one more example of the past perfect continuous, the past perfect simple and the past perfect passive.

Book review – *The Incredible Journey*

c Complete the text with the correct form of the past perfect continuous, the past perfect simple or the past perfect passive. There may be more than one possibility.

The Incredible Journey is a story about two dogs and a cat in Canada who found themselves far from their home. Their owners, the Hunter family, had gone to live in England for a short time, and so the three pets ¹......*had been taken*..... (take) to live on a farm owned by a friend, Mr Longridge. The animals did not really understand what ² .... (happen), and they patiently waited for their owners to come and get them. They began to think that maybe they ³ .... (forget) by the Hunters. After about two weeks – during which time they ⁴ .... (treat) well by Mr Longridge – the animals decided that they had waited long enough. They left the farm and started to walk back home, following their instincts. But they didn't know that their journey would take them across 400 kilometres!

The story tells us of this amazing journey. When they finally got home, the animals ⁵ .... (travel) for many weeks and ⁶ .... (had) many difficult experiences. They ⁷ .... (face) starvation, illness and had been attacked by wild animals. And of course their owners, who ⁸ .... (tell) that they were missing and who ⁹ .... (look) for them, were pleased to have them back again.

This is a moving story about animal courage and instincts.

3 Listen

a Match the words with the pictures.

cricket chameleon shark butterfly silkworm

  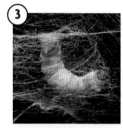 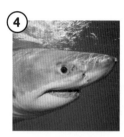 

1 .... 2 .... 3 .... 4 .... 5 ....

b Match the words 1–5 with statements a–g There are two statements that you won't use.

1 Crickets
2 Chameleons
3 Butterflies
4 Sharks
5 Silkworms

a use the antennae on their heads to listen and communicate.
b use smell to find a partner.
c use their legs to listen.
d hear by picking up sound vibrations from a membrane on their legs.
e have eyes that can look in different directions at the same time.
f use their feet to taste things.
g can detect the presence of other animals through electric charges.

c 🔊 Listen to the radio quiz to check your answers.

d 🔊 Listen again. Who wins the quiz? Tick (✓) the correct box.

Gillian ☐   Scott ☐

4 Vocabulary

Animal sounds

a 🔊 Listen to the animal sounds. Match the pictures a–g with the sounds 1–7.

1 bark   5 crow
2 roar   6 hiss
3 croak   7 grunt
4 bleat

b The verbs from Exercise 4a are sometimes used to describe human speech. Complete the sentences using the correct verb from Exercise 4a.

1 The football coach ___barked___ his instructions to the players.
2 They all _____ with laughter when they saw what I was wearing.
3 My father didn't actually say 'Yes', he just _____ .
4 The actors were terrible and the audience _____ their disapproval.
5 Harry just about managed to _____ that he was OK although he had a very sore throat.
6 He won the school tennis championship and _____ about it for weeks.
7 I hate it when she _____ on about how badly everyone treats her.

5 Read and speak

a Work in a group of three. Read a different story each and then re-tell the story to your group, using your own words.

(1)

Alfie saves the day!

A Philadelphia family's dog is being acclaimed as a hero after sounding the alert when he saw the family's two-year-old child playing on the roof. As his parents slept, toddler Philip Redman crawled through a broken window and onto the roof of their home with Alfie, the family dog, following close behind him. Family members say the boy's parents had placed a playpen in front of the broken window to keep Philip safe. But little Philip was able to move the playpen and climb out of the window.

Alfie followed Philip out of the window and began barking. It was his barking that drew the attention of neighbours and Philip's sleeping parents.

(2)

Cat's amazing journey

A two-year-old cat called Kuzya has made an amazing journey across Siberia.

The cat's owners moved from the small village of Olenyok to the city of Yakutsk taking their pet with them. Unfortunately Kuzya didn't like his new home and walked 2,150 kilometres to get back to Olenyok. He appeared on the doorstep of the old family home three months later, looking unfed and wild. 'There were teeth marks on the cat's tail. Now he's very nervous and is always looking for a hiding place. The poor animal had to cross woods, hills, rivers and lakes. It's simply unbelievable,' said a family member.

(3)

Terriers save their owners from fire

Two Jack Russell terriers called Barbie and Lucy are being honoured as heroes in Gainesville, Florida after waking up their two human guardians and alerting them to a fire. Richard Pla and Kyle Strohmann were woken up around 8.30am on Christmas Eve by the sound of the dogs barking to discover their house was on fire. Thanks to the early warning, the men were able to escape with only minor burns and smoke inhalation.

According to Richard, the dogs gave them 'just about the 30 seconds we needed to get up, get to the front door and get ourselves and the dogs out to safety before the house burst into flames'.

b In what ways are these animals heroes?

c In your group, tell each other similar stories you have heard about animals behaving in a heroic way.

Literature in mind

6 Read

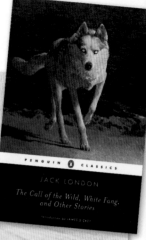

(a) Look at the cover of the book and read the short summary of the story. Would you be interested in reading this book? Why / Why not?

(b) Read the text below quickly to find the answers to these questions.

1 What happens to Buck's sense of smell and hearing? Give examples.

2 What examples are there of the 'instincts long dead' that came alive again in Buck?

Buck is born to a life of luxury, but he's betrayed by an estate gardener in California who sells him as a sledge dog to Alaska. During the time of the famous Klondike Gold Rush in 1897 dogs like Buck are in great demand in the frozen north. In his new environment, Buck's primitive, wolf-like nature gradually begins to emerge. Buck escapes, courageously fighting for survival, and finally leads a pack of wolves and becomes a legend of the north.

THE CALL OF THE WILD
by Jack London

Not that Buck reasoned it out. He was fit that was all, and unconsciously he adjusted himself to the new mode of life. All his days, no matter what the odds, he had never run from a fight. But the stick of the man in the red sweater had beaten into him a more fundamental and primitive code. He now ran away to save his hide. He did not steal for joy of it, but because of the noise of his stomach. He did not rob openly, but stole secretly and cunningly, out of respect for the stick and fang. In short, the things he did were done because it was easier to do them than not to do them.

His development (or retrogression) was rapid. His muscles became hard as iron, and he grew indifferent to all ordinary pain. He achieved an internal as well as external economy. He could eat anything, no matter how loathsome or indigestible; and, once eaten, the juices of his stomach extracted the last least particle of nutrition; and his blood carried it to the farthest reaches of his body, building it into the toughest and stoutest of tissues. Sight and scent became remarkably keen while his hearing developed such acuteness that in his sleep he heard the faintest sound and knew whether it heralded peace or peril. He learned to bite the ice out with his teeth when it collected between his toes; and when he was thirsty and there was a thick layer of ice over the water hole, he would break it by rearing and striking it with stiff fore legs. His most obvious trait was an ability to scent the wind and forecast it a night in advance. No matter how breathless the air when he dug his nest by tree or bank, the wind that later blew inevitably found him sheltered and snug.

And not only did he learn by experience, but instincts long dead came alive again. The domesticated generations fell from him. In vague ways he remembered back to the youth of the breed, to the time the wild dogs moved in packs through the primeval forest and killed their meat as they ran it down. It was no task for him to learn to fight like a wolf. In this manner forgotten ancestors had fought. They stimulated the old life within him, and the old tricks which they had stamped into the heredity of the breed were his tricks. They came to him without effort or discovery, as though they had been his always. And when, on the still cold nights, he pointed his nose at a star and howled long and wolflike, it was his ancestors, dead and dust, pointing nose at star and howling down through the centuries and through him. And his cadences were their cadences, the cadences which voiced their sadness and what to them was the meaning of the stiffness, and the cold, and dark.

(c) Use a dictionary to find the meanings of expressions 1–8 from the text. Explain them in your own words.

1 reasoned it out (paragraph 1)
tried to understand something to make a judgement

2 no matter what the odds (paragraph 1)

3 save his hide (paragraph 1)

4 farthest reaches (paragraph 2)

5 stoutest of tissues (paragraph 2)

6 fell from him (paragraph 3)

7 ran it down (paragraph 3)

8 heredity of the breed (paragraph 3)

(d) Find words in the text with these meanings.

1 in good physical condition (paragraph 1)
fit

2 tooth (paragraph 1)

3 awful (paragraph 2)

4 sharpness (paragraph 2)

5 danger (paragraph 2)

6 comfortable and warm (paragraph 2)

7 groups of dogs or wolves (paragraph 3)

8 quality of one's personality taken from past generations (paragraph 3)

7 Write

a Read the magazine article quickly to find the answers to these questions.

1 How did the narrator feel when Goldie first came to her house?

2 What was Goldie's behaviour like in her first few days at the narrator's house?

3 Why did Goldie bolt off to a farmhouse one day?

b Work with a partner. Read the magazine article again and discuss the questions.

1 How does the writer create a strong opening to the article?

2 How does the writer continue to hold the reader's attention?

3 What makes the ending particularly effective?

c Read the article again. Find examples of techniques 1–4 which help to hold a reader's attention when reading a story.

1 interesting descriptions and use of vocabulary to describe people, places and animals

2 direct speech

3 building up tension by giving hints as to what might happen later

4 interesting psychological insights into someone's thoughts and feelings

d Write an article about animals for the magazine. Before you start writing, think about:

● What is your storyline going to be?

● How can you use techniques 1–4 from Exercise 7c to create an interesting article?

● How will you create a strong opening and ending of the article?

Goldie's Secret

She showed up at the doorstep of my house in Cornwall. No way could I have sent her away. No way, not me anyway. Maybe someone had kicked her out of their car the night before. 'We're moving house.' 'No space for her any more with the baby coming.' 'We never really wanted her, but what could we have done? She was a present.' People find all sorts of excuses for abandoning an animal. And she was one of the most beautiful animals I had ever seen, a magnificent Golden Retriever.

I called her Goldie, which was not the most creative choice of names, I know. Who knows, maybe if I had known what was going to happen I would have given her a more dramatic name. She was so unsettled during those first few days. She hardly ate anything and had such an air of sadness about her. There was nothing I could do to make her happy, it seemed. Heaven knows what had happened to her at her previous owners. But eventually at the end of the first week she calmed down and became as loyal and loving as an animal could be. Always by my side, whether we were out on one of our long walks or sitting snugly by the fire.

That's why it was such a shock when she pulled away from me one day when we were out for a walk. We were a long way from home, when she started barking and getting very agitated. Eventually I couldn't hold her any longer and she raced off down the road and over a ditch towards a farmhouse in the distance as fast as her legs could carry her.

By the time I reached the farm I was exhausted, red in the face and very upset with Goldie. But when I saw her licking and fussing round the four Retriever puppies my heart melted. 'We didn't know what had happened to her,' said the woman at the door. 'I took her for a walk one day, soon after the puppies were born, and she just disappeared.' 'She must have tried to come back to them and got lost,' added a boy from behind her.

I must admit I do miss Goldie, but I've got Nugget now, and she looks just like her mother. And I've learnt a good lesson: not to judge people.

2 Snap decisions

* Future in the past
* Vocabulary: making decisions

1 Read and listen

(a) 🔊 Listen to the four musical clips and write down if you think a man or woman is playing the instrument. Compare your ideas with a partner.

(b) Read the text quickly to find the answers to these questions.

1 Who was playing?
2 Who were the listeners?
3 What does the title 'Listening with your eyes' mean?

Listening with your eyes

I never cease to be amazed by the assumptions people make and the prejudices they hold, and recently I heard a story that, for me, summed up just how misguided some firmly held beliefs can be. The story was about a person called Abbie Conant – a professional musician living in Italy and looking to move on from playing the trombone for the Royal Opera of Turin. Following 11 applications for openings in orchestras throughout Europe, only one responded: the Munich Philharmonic Orchestra. Abbie Conant received a letter from them which began, 'Dear Mr Conant,' before going on to include an invitation to an audition.

Apparently, the audition in June 1980 took place in a museum, since the usual venue, the orchestra's cultural centre, was unavailable. There were over 30 candidates that day and each one played their piece behind a screen, meaning the selection committee never actually saw the individuals concerned: they only heard them play. Conant, candidate number 16, played Ferdinand David's *Konzertino for Trombone*, a standard piece for auditions. Being a perfectionist, Conant was annoyed with herself for missing a note in the piece, and was seen packing the trombone away immediately after the audition in preparation to leave.

But the selection committee, who were trained to identify brilliant musicians in seconds flat, knew instantly that Conant was the best of all the people they'd heard that day. Their decision was easy – they asked the other candidates to leave and someone went to find Conant and impart the good news.

However, events took an unexpected turn: the selection committee were waiting, sure they were going to be introduced to the brilliant Mr Conant, when in walked a woman! The committee members were astounded! The whole idea of a female lead trombonist went against

tradition, but Abbie Conant had proved them wrong and shattered their prejudices. Or had she?

There were two more sets of auditions (not behind screens this time), and I gather Conant passed both with flying colours. Yet still the orchestra leaders weren't happy. Personally, I think Conant's outstanding ability posed a real dilemma for the orchestra leaders because it made them question themselves.

Nonetheless, Conant joined the orchestra and played her probationary year successfully. But then she found out that she was going to be demoted to second trombone, basically because she was female.

Understandably, Conant took the orchestra to court to fight the case, and despite the orchestra's claims that Abbie Conant was not strong enough to play first trombone, she won her case. It took her years to prove herself in the eyes of the law, but she did it and she was reinstated as first trombone.

> "She knew she would win, and she did."

I thought that was the end of the story – but, no. The orchestra then refused to pay Conant the same as her male colleagues, so she took them to court again. She knew she would win, and she did. The basis of her victory was this: the committee had chosen Conant under unbiased conditions, hearing her play from behind a screen and thus judging her on her ability, not her sex. At last, the prejudices and assumptions of the orchestra were finally negated. In fact, you could say Abbie Conant was saved by the screen.

I have since heard that the Munich Philharmonic Orchestra has never auditioned people behind a screen again!

c) 🔊 Read the text again and listen. Answer the questions.

1 Under what conditions was the first round of auditions held?
2 What did Abbie Conant think of her performance in the first round of auditions and what reactions did she get from the selection committee?
3 What was the unexpected turn of events that shocked the committee?
4 Why does the writer think the orchestra leaders felt uncomfortable about Conant doing so well in all the auditions?
5 Ms Conant took the case to court twice. Why did she do so and what were the outcomes?
6 What is meant by '... Abbie Conant was saved by the screen'?

d) Find words and expressions in the text that mean:

1 unfair and unreasonable opinions or feelings, especially when formed without enough thought or knowledge (paragraph 1)
2 jobs or opportunities to do something (paragraph 1)
3 a short performance in which actors or musicians show their capabilities when they apply for a position in an orchestra (paragraph 1)
4 a vertical structure which is used to separate one area from another (paragraph 2)
5 extremely surprised (paragraph 4)
6 performed very successfully in an exam (paragraph 5)
7 given a less important position (paragraph 6)
8 given back their previous job or position (paragraph 7)
9 not influenced by one's own opinions (paragraph 8)

2 Listen and speak

a) In paragraph 3 of the text it says the selection committee made their decision 'in seconds flat'. What do you think 'in seconds flat' means?

b) 🔊 Listen to the people talking about making 'snap decisions' and write a definition of the term using your own words.

c) What positive and negative examples are given?

d) Think of a time when you made a snap decision. Tell a partner.

Discussion box

Work in pairs or small groups. Discuss these questions together.

1 In modern society, do men and women have equal rights?
2 Do you think men and women have different qualities or is this a stereotype?
3 Think of jobs or hobbies you associate with being either very male or female. Why is this? What improvements to the job/hobby would the other sex make?

3 Grammar

Future in the past

a) Look at these examples.

*They were sure they **were going to meet** Mr Conant, but in walked a woman.*

*She **was going to be demoted** to second trombone.*

*She knew she **would** win.*

Rule:
- When we talk about the future, we can use *be going to* (for plans, intentions and processes) or *will* (for predictions).
- When we want to talk about the future as seen from a time in the past, we can use _____ / _____ going to or _____ .

b) Complete the following sentences with the correct form of the future in the past: *was/were going to* or *would*. Sometimes there is more than one answer.

1 The computer company announced that the new software *was going to be released* (release) in the first half of next year.
2 Phil and Paul knew the job _____ (not/be) easy but they didn't expect it to be that hard.
3 The local people thought it _____ (be) a shame not to build the bridge across the river.
4 The young prisoner who managed to escape _____ (release) next month.
5 I saw the laptop that you _____ (buy) in a big advert in the newspaper.
6 He probably thought there _____ (be) less risk of upsetting me if he didn't tell me personally, so he sent me an email.

c) We often use *was/were going to ...* to say that the planned future action didn't happen:

I was going to phone you, but I forgot.

Work with a partner. Talk about things you were going to do in the past but didn't do. Explain why you didn't do them.

4 Listen

(a) 🔊 Listen to the radio programme. Did the book reviewers enjoy *Blink*?

(b) 🔊 Listen again and choose the correct answers, a, b or c.

1 *Blink* is about
  a making split-second decisions.
  b the importance of thinking things over.
  c the relationship between blinking an eye and human thinking.

2 Before Claire read the book she thought that
  a decisions should be made based on instincts.
  b we need to think seriously and carefully before making a decision.
  c she would really enjoy it.

3 The example of the Cook County Hospital shows that doctors can diagnose patients better if they
  a focus on very few, but critical pieces of information about the patient.
  b take the patient's blood pressure before they look into their medical history.
  c analyse as much information about the patient as possible.

4 US companies often make mistakes in choosing the right people for CEOs because they
  a do not consider that there is a link between height and intelligence.
  b seem to prefer choosing tall people for leadership roles.
  c do not trust their rapid cognition skills when choosing effective leaders.

(c) 🔊 Listen again. Which of the speakers Brian, Anne or Claire:

1 believes they are not very skilled at making decisions?
2 had initial doubts about *Blink*, but seems to have changed their beliefs about decision making?
3 claims it is an example of bad recognition that CEOs of top US companies are often tall?
4 enjoyed reading the book the least?

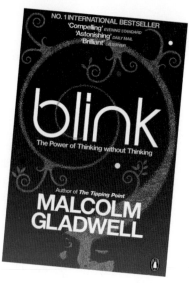

5 Vocabulary

Making decisions

(a) Match the two parts of the sentences.

1 It was a split-
2 Why do you always jump
3 Come on. Make
4 It's difficult to make
5 It was a snap
6 He spent hours dithering
7 Why don't you mull
8 We've come to

  a your mind up. We haven't got all day.
  b judgement and it was wrong.
  c second decision and it saved his life.
  d things over and give me an answer tomorrow?
  e to the wrong conclusion?
  f a decision and you're not going to like it.
  g an informed decision with so few facts.
  h over his decision and still made the wrong one.

(b) Replace the words in *italics* and brackets with words from the box.

> dither   an informed decision   snap   making your mind up   jumping to the wrong conclusion   ~~split-second decisions~~   mull things over

> Are you good at making (very quick decisions) [1] *split-second decisions* or do you (hesitate and change your mind) [2] _____ for ages before (coming to a decision) [3] _____ ? Most people like to have enough time to (think about things well) [4] _____ and gather enough facts to make (a decision based on facts) [5] _____ . Don't let your indecision get in your way. Become a confident decision-maker and learn to make those all-important (quick) [6] _____ judgements without (making a quick but incorrect decision) [7] _____ . **Contact Decision Makers...**

6 **Read and speak**

a Read the three scenarios and decide what you would do in each situation.

Scenario 1

You are walking your dog along the pier. Your dog falls into the water chasing a ball you have thrown for him. You are a good swimmer. You are on your own but there are other people on the pier. You do not have a mobile phone with you. You live 15 minutes' drive from the beach. Your dog can paddle, but the current is extremely strong around the pier and he is being pulled under. What do you do?

1   Dive in and try to rescue your dog
2   Borrow someone's mobile phone and call your parents or a friend
3   Borrow someone's mobile phone and call the emergency services

Scenario 2

The last train home is leaving the platform at the very moment you get to the station. You haven't got much money, you haven't got your mobile phone with you, and it's late. What do you do?

1   Run after the train, hoping it will stop (it's still on the platform and only moving slowly)
2   Go out of the station and see if there's a bus
3   Get a taxi home, hoping that your parents will pay for it when you get home

Scenario 3

You go for a walk on the beach with your friend. The tide is out and you are walking towards an island that is now connected to the mainland. You have an argument and your friend walks off on their own. After a while you realise the tide is coming in fast and the island is about to be cut off. Your friend doesn't seem to have noticed. What do you do?

1   Run out after your friend
2   Run up to the coastguard
3   Nothing. You are still angry with your friend

b Work in a small group. Discuss the consequences of each decision, and decide which is the best one for each scenario.

Speaking

7 Speak and listen

(a) Work with a partner. Look at the three photographs, and decide what they have got in common. What is different about each one? Think about each situation and what is happening.

(b) 🔊 Listen to three interviews. Which of the situations from Exercise 7a is each interview from? Write in the boxes.

Interview 1 ☐
Interview 2 ☐
Interview 3 ☐

(c) 🔊 Which phrases are said by an interviewer and which are said by an interviewee? Mark the phrases *I* (interviewer) or *Ie* (interviewee).

1 Perhaps you could tell us *I*
2 Let me think a moment.
3 It's a bit of a long story.
4 I think I'd have to say …
5 I don't really know what to tell you.
6 Tell us a bit about yourself.
7 Let's talk a bit, if we may, …
8 Would you mind if I asked you …
9 Sure, fire away.
10 Just give me a moment, OK.

Listen and check your answers.

(d) Read the phrases in Exercise 7c again. Decide whether each one is formal, informal or neutral.

(e) Work with a partner. One of you is going to interview the other. Before you start, talk about each situation and decide if it is formal or informal. Where will each interview take place? Think of six possible questions together. Change roles for the second activity.

1 You are doing a market survey to find out about people's computer use. Find out if they use computers for work or pleasure, how long they spend on a computer every day, what type of things they do on their computer and any other useful information.

2 You are the manager in a pizzeria and you are interviewing someone for a part-time job as a waiter. Find out what experience they have, their availability and try to decide if they are suitable for the job.

8 Pronunciation

Sounding polite or angry

🔊 Turn to page 122.

9 Write

a Read the letter below to find the answer to the question.

1　What was the attitude of the assistants in the camera shop?

b Read the letter again and match the titles A–C with the paragraphs. Write A–C in the spaces.

A letter of complaint needs to give:

A　details of what happened

B　a clear statement as to what is expected from the addressee

C　an overall idea of what the complaint is all about

c Read the letter again. What techniques does the writer use to make her letter convincing?

d How does the writer convey to the reader how she felt and is feeling about the situation she is describing?

e Replace the underlined informal language with the correct formal phrase from the box.

> express my annoyance　discovered　have no objection to
> would like to point out　it is my opinion　dismayed
> wish　am not prepared to

1　I am writing to <u>tell you I'm cross</u> about your new payment structure.

2　I <u>don't want to</u> be a part of such a disorganised business venture.

3　I <u>want</u> to report one of your members of staff.

4　I was <u>upset</u> to see you hadn't carried out my instructions.

5　<u>I think</u> that you should provide sufficient car parking outside the school.

6　I <u>want to say</u> that we have always paid our bills on time.

7　I <u>don't mind</u> you leaving work at 4pm as long as you work a seven-hour day.

8　My colleague <u>found out</u> that you don't have a licence to sell alcohol on the premises.

f Think of a negative experience you've had with a shop assistant or manager. Write a letter of complaint to the person or their superior. Keep to the structure of the letter below and use as many of the phrases from Exercise 9e as you can.

Dear Sir/Madam,

1 ☐
I am writing to express my annoyance at the quality of service offered in your shop in Cornmarket Street in Oxford. I have been a loyal customer for many years and am deeply disappointed at having to write this letter.

2 ☐
I went into the shop on 15 July to buy a Virtual Focus digital camera. Not only were the assistants totally uninformed about the product but they were also unhelpful and rude. They were unable to answer specific questions and when I asked if the camera had auto focus, one of your staff, Jeremy Baldwin, replied 'How should I know?' Later, I was appalled when I overheard him saying to a colleague: 'She'd be better off buying a washing machine than a digital camera!' Needless to say, I find this type of attitude totally unacceptable.

3 ☐
I think you can understand perfectly why I left your shop immediately, and will not be buying any more of your products unless I receive an official apology from the sales team in the shop. I would further like to stress that should I not hear from you, I will write a letter to the editor of the *Oxford Daily Messenger* in the hope that I can save others from similarly humiliating experiences.

Yours faithfully,
Marianne Crombe

③ Advertising

* Position of adverbs
* Vocabulary: advertising

1 Read and listen

(a) Look at the adverts a–c. What are they for? How effective are they?

(b) Read the text quickly to find the answers to these questions.

1 Find three examples of things people buy because price and quality are considerations.

2 Find three examples of things people buy because they are influenced by their emotions.

(c) 🔊 Read the text again. Which of Mark Stanton's replies A–D mentions these points?

1 As we get older we get better at convincing ourselves that we need to have a particular product.

2 We more commonly use logic to buy commodities.

3 We use logic to try and make ourselves feel better about making a purchase.

4 Marketing people need to appeal to emotions such as happiness, fear and anger.

5 Young people are most likely to make decisions solely based on emotion.

6 Logic is used when we want to get value for money from a product.

7 Being able to relate to how people are feeling is an excellent skill for life.

8 Emotion is the most important factor in our decision to buy something.

Sharper than you think. The WMF Grand Gourmet knife with Damasteel blade.

Advertising: the logic of emotions

What is it that makes us buy the things we buy? Why do we go for one product over another? Do we usually shop with our head or our heart? Mark Stanton, a leading marketing consultant, joins us to answer these questions and to shed light on our purchasing habits.

MoneyMag: It's often said that people decide what to buy emotionally, and then use logic to justify their decision. But is this actually true?

(A) Mark Stanton: Yes, it is. We all fundamentally make our decisions based on emotion, not logic. Logic supports our emotions and is used to justify our decisions after we've made them. It plays a part, but emotion is the core ingredient. The product that people can't get excited about won't sell. Likewise, the ad that doesn't provoke emotion won't work.

MoneyMag: But can a product be sold on emotion alone?

(B) Mark Stanton: Yes, but this happens most commonly with children. Children desperately want to fit in. The easiest way to entice a child is to present your product as the one purchase that every other kid on the block is getting. It is just what they need to be like everyone else. Does anyone truthfully need shoes that light up at each step? The answer's no, unless you're a kid and all your friends have got them. And if it weren't for other people wanting it, could there be any justification for mobile phone wallpaper?

When I was a child, everybody had streamers; long strips of coloured plastic which you attached to the handlebars on your bicycle. They flapped around in the breeze and were absolutely useless except to show all the other kids that you had them.

Of course, older kids, even sixty-year-old kids, are sometimes under pressure to fit in. The only difference is they've become much better at justifying their purchase choices. They've learned to convince themselves that they really do need a faster car or a bigger lawn mower, for example. The truth is, they obviously don't.

MoneyMag: What about the other extreme? Can a product be sold purely on logic alone?

(C) Mark Stanton: Surprisingly, the answer is yes, but only if it's an interchangeable, mass-produced, unspecialised product like petrol, rice or airline seats. We buy them from a strictly transactional point of view by dividing benefits by price. More benefits, lower price, better deal. But, for everything else we buy, emotion plays a major part in our decisions.

d (Circle) the correct preposition to complete the verb for the meaning given. Then read the text to check your answers.

1 to go (for) / on / about something over another – to choose one thing instead of another

2 to shed light *above / over / on* something – to explain further and make clearer

3 to fit *out / in / on* – to be accepted as part of a group

4 to figure *up / out / over* – to understand

5 to back *in / up / over* your appeal – to support

6 to be *on / up / out* to a winner – to be in an extremely good situation

---

MoneyMag: So what does all this mean for advertisers? What do they need to make a good ad?

(D) Mark Stanton: Well, the answer is surprisingly simple: a combination of both emotion and logic. You need to figure out what your customers are emotional about: what they love, and what they hate, what keeps them awake at night, what gives them ulcers and what catastrophic events they dread. If you appeal to those emotions and back up your appeal with solid facts you will surely be on to a winner.

All great leaders and managers, all great marketeers, all great teachers and all great product designers learn how to harmonise with the emotions of the people they work with and turn them on and off at will. This, of all things, is the greatest and most profitable art form in marketing, and always will be. And it is one of the most valuable skills we will learn in life.

c

---

2 Grammar
Position of adverbs

a Read the basic rules on positions of adverbs in sentences. Then match sentences 1–6 with the rules. Write the number of the most relevant rule in the box.

1 We often use an adverb to add extra meaning to an adjective. This is also called *qualifying an adjective*. In this case the adverb comes before the adjective.

2 When we use an adverb to qualify a verb, it can go before the verb (but after the verb *to be*).

3 Adverbs normally don't go between a verb and its object.

4 We sometimes put adverbs at the beginning of a sentence to qualify the whole idea of the sentence.

5 Adverbs can come at the end of clauses when they qualify a more complex idea.

6 Adverbial phrases normally come at the end of clauses.

a Children desperately want to fit in.   `2`

b Surprisingly, the answer is yes. ☐

c You have to present the product in an interesting way. ☐

d The answer is surprisingly simple. ☐

e It's often said that people decide what to buy emotionally. ☐

f NOT ~~Read quickly the text~~. ☐

Discussion box

Work in pairs or small groups. Discuss these questions together.

1 Think of some things you've bought. Did you use logic or emotion in your decision to buy them?

2 What are some of your favourite adverts and why do you like them?

3 What are some of your least favourite adverts and what don't you like about them?

---

c Complete the sentences with the adverb in brackets. Do not add any commas or change punctuation. There may be more than one answer.

1 It was a fascinating film. (really)
   It was a really fascinating film.

2 I didn't enjoy the meal. (really)

3 Buying something is a personal decision. (clearly)

4 We thought about it before deciding. (carefully)

5 I bought the wrong thing. (unfortunately)

6 I don't know the answer. (honestly)

7 He showed us the medal he'd won. (proudly)

8 She showed me how to do it. (in an interesting way)

d Work with a partner. Discuss your answers and decide how many correct options there are for each sentence. Match each sentence from Exercise 2c to a rule in Exercise 2a.

3 Vocabulary

Advertising

(a) Match the words with the pictures. Write 1–6 in the boxes.

1 hoarding	3 slogan	5 sandwich board
2 jingle	4 logos	6 TV commercial

(b) Work with a partner and discuss these questions.

1 How effective are each of the types of advertising in Exercise 3a?
2 What other forms of advertising can you think of?
3 Does advertising ever annoy you? When and why?

4 Listen

(a) What are the differences between internet adverts and adverts in magazines?

(b) What are pop-ups and where would you expect to see them?

(c) 🔊 What does the expert say are the differences between internet adverts and adverts in magazines? List three differences.

(d) 🔊 Listen and complete the notes.

A career in advertising? Is this really for me?

* It's a good idea to study ¹_____ at university.
* The most important part of an online ad is the ²_____ - this must be good to grab the ³_____ of the people who see it.
* A lot of people have a ⁴_____ impression of online ads because they think they are ⁵_____ - it's a big challenge to change this conception.
* It's difficult to ⁶_____ pop-ups because they cover your computer ⁷_____ - this doesn't mean they are a good method of advertising. (I hate them!!!!)
* Not many people ⁸_____ pop-ups and those that do don't ⁹_____ them.
* Internet adverts can use loads of different ways to get their message across like ¹⁰_____, ¹¹_____ and ¹²_____ (and some others that I can't remember).
* Remember the golden rule AIDA - that is, Attention, ¹³_____, Desire and ¹⁴_____

5 Grammar

Adjective order

(a) If we have more than one adjective to qualify a noun, there are some basic guidelines to follow about the order they come in. Look at the examples and complete the rule.

*On the screen, you get **annoying multi-coloured** pop-ups.*

*Let's have a **nice loud** round of applause for Steve Wilson.*

> **Rule:**
> • If one adjective gives an opinion and the other one gives a fact, the .... comes first.

(b) 🔊 Listen to the sentences and complete the table. Fill in the four category titles in the box in the correct order. Then complete the examples from the sentences.

colour   material   origin   shape

Quality					Noun
gorgeous		dark brown			jacket
	round				cakes
			Italian		garden
				pearl	necklace
					elephant
					frame

(c) Write the adjectives in the correct order before the nouns.

1 a jacket *leather / beautiful*
   A beautiful leather jacket
2 a book *reference / useful*
3 the cup *old / plastic*
4 eyes *blue / beautiful*
5 a car *expensive / sports / German*
6 shoes *running / comfortable / Chinese*
7 my shirt *white / best / cotton*
8 a company *advertising / enormous / American*

(d) Think of some adjectives that you could use to describe these nouns. Write a sentence using the adjectives and noun. Use a dictionary if you need to.

1 a book
   An interesting little book
2 a programme
3 a room
4 a building
5 a pen
6 a jacket

6 Speak

(a) Work in small groups. You are designing a marketing campaign for a product of your choice. Use the following guidelines to help you.

• What is your product? (use a real one or an imaginary one)
• Who is your target audience?
• What market research would you ideally do before designing your campaign?
• What different types of advertising are you going to use?
• Design the actual adverts you will use.

(b) Present your ideas to the rest of the class. Choose a member of the group to do each of the following:

• Introduce your product and explain who you think will be interested in it and why.
• Explain the different areas of the media you will target and why.
• Show any visual adverts you might have and explain the ideas behind them.
• Act out any TV or radio commercials you might have.

Culture in mind

I shop therefore I am

7 Read and speak

(a) Work with a partner. Look at the image and discuss what it means. Is it true for you?

(b) Read the text quickly and define 'Buy Nothing Day' in your own words.

the ultimate refund

1

On 24 and 25 November, the busiest days in the American retail calendar and the unofficial start of the international Christmas shopping season, thousands of activists and concerned citizens in 65 countries will take a 24-hour consumer detox as part of the 14th annual Buy Nothing Day, a global phenomenon that originated in Vancouver, Canada.

2

From joining zombie marches through malls to organising credit card 'cut-ups' and shopaholic clinics, Buy Nothing Day activists aim to challenge themselves, their families and their friends to switch off from shopping and tune back into life for one day. Featured in recent years by the likes of CNN, Wired, the BBC, and the CBC, the global event is celebrated as a relaxed family holiday, as a non-commercial street party, or even as a politically charged public protest. Anyone can take part provided they spend a day without spending.

3

Reasons for participating in Buy Nothing Day are as varied as the people who choose to participate. Some see it as an escape from the marketing mind games and frantic consumer binge that has come to characterise the holiday season, and our culture in general. Others use it to expose the environmental and ethical consequences of over-consumption.

4

Two recent, high-profile disaster warnings outline the sudden urgency of our dilemma. First of all, in October, a global warming report by economist Sir Nicholas Stern predicted that climate change will lead to the most massive and most wide-ranging market failure the world has ever seen. Soon afterwards, a major study published in the journal Science forecasted the near-total collapse of global fisheries within 40 years.

Kalle Lasn, co-founder of the Adbusters Media Foundation, which was responsible for turning Buy Nothing Day into an international annual event, said: 'Our headlong plunge into ecological collapse requires a profound shift in the way we see things. Driving hybrid cars and limiting industrial emissions is great, but they are band-aid solutions if we don't address the core problem: we have to consume less. This is the message of Buy Nothing Day.'

5

As Lasn suggests, Buy Nothing Day isn't just about changing your habits for one day. It's about starting a lasting lifestyle commitment to consuming less and producing less waste. With six billion people on the planet, it's the responsibility of the most affluent – the upper 20 per cent that consumes 80 per cent of the world's resources – to begin setting the example.

(c) Match the titles A–E with the paragraphs. Write A–E in the spaces.

A   Why people take part
B   Not just one day
C   Events
D   The underlying message
E   Buy Nothing Day

(d) Write the paragraph number next to the relevant quotes. One paragraph is not used.

1   'Yes, we had a great day, the kids came, there was street music, and we met lots of other people.' ☐

2   'Well, we're definitely going to start thinking about how we can change our day-to-day lives.' ☐

3   'If we keep exploiting our natural resources at the rate we're doing currently, we'll soon run out of basic commodities such as oil, fresh water and food.' ☐

4   'I suppose because I believe we need to do something to show we care about the environment.' ☐

(e) Work with a partner to write questions that correspond to the quotations 1–4 in Exercise 7d.

Discussion box

Work in pairs or small groups and discuss these topics together.

1 Think of ways you can consume less and still enjoy yourself:
   - at Christmas
   - on Valentine's Day
   - on a relative's birthday
   - in the summer holidays

2 Think of how you could realistically consume less.

8 Write

a Read the job advertisement. Write a list of the personal qualities a successful candidate should possess.

PR Assistant

Have you got the energy and enthusiasm to get ahead in the world of marketing?

We are a leading advertising agency based in Manchester. We are looking for a young motivated PR assistant to support our creative team. This role is incredibly busy and not for the faint-hearted. You will be responsible for the team diaries, travel arrangements, PowerPoint presentations and general administration. The successful candidate will be open, dynamic and willing to learn. Experience is not essential but advanced knowledge of MS Office is an advantage.

If you are interested and think you have got what we are looking for, then send us a CV with a short covering letter telling us why you think you are right for the job.

b Complete the list of points to include in a covering letter.

1 Where you saw the advertisement.
2 Why you want to apply for this job.
3 ....
4 ....
5 ....

c Read through the model letter and check your answers to Exercise 8b.

Dear Sir/Madam,

I am writing to apply for the job as PR Assistant that was advertised in last night's Evening Standard. Please also find enclosed a copy of my CV. As you will see, I graduated in administration from Bradford University and have spent the last two years working for a small, but dynamic publishing house in London. Although I have enjoyed my time here and learned many things, I feel I have reached a point where I need to prove myself at a higher level. I am sure I can offer you the enthusiasm and dedication to the task that you are looking for. I am good at working under pressure, indeed you might say I thrive on it, and would enjoy the challenge of using my skills in a larger environment.

I hope I have convinced you that I am a suitable candidate for the post.

I look forward to hearing from you.

Yours faithfully,

Sally Dixon

d Choose one of the job adverts and write a covering letter of application.

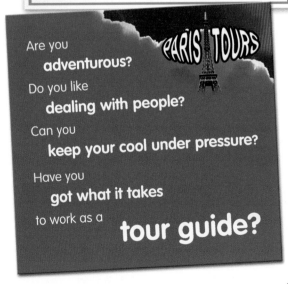

Do you have a way with words?

Yes? Well, we're looking for creative and motivated people interested in starting a career in advertising.

PARIS TOURS

Are you **adventurous?**

Do you like **dealing with people?**

Can you **keep your cool under pressure?**

Have you **got what it takes** to work as a **tour guide?**

For your portfolio

4 Fight or flight?

* Talking about tendencies
* Vocabulary: feeling stressed
* Vocabulary: coping with stress

1 Listen

(a) Look at the pictures and describe what's happening. Which caveman do you identify with most?

(b) 🔊 Listen to the beginning of a magazine article. Which picture in Exercise 1a does it describe?

(c) 🔊 Listen again and make notes about what happens to the caveman's body and physical abilities.

2 Read and listen

(a) In your own words, define a 'sabre-tooth tiger' situation.

(b) Work with a partner. Think of some 'sabre-tooth tiger' situations in modern life.

(c) Read the next part of the magazine article quickly. How many of your 'sabre-tooth tiger' situations does it mention?

Flash forward to the present day. Despite the huge amount of technological change in the ensuing 25,000 years, you are still walking around with essentially the same set of internal body parts as the caveman. At this very moment you're thirsty and hunting for something to drink. So you start walking towards the drinks machine at school. Your teacher is out hunting too. But guess what? She's hunting for you.

As you gulp down your can of cola you hear your teacher say those dreaded words: 'Could I see you for a moment in the classroom, please?' At the sight of the tiger (or rather, your teacher), your hypothalamus gland sends a message to your adrenal glands and within seconds your body summons all the same powers that your stone age ancestor needed to fight a sabre-tooth tiger.

You can almost feel your blood pressure soar as you take the long walk down the corridor to your English class. She's always picking on you. What can it be this time? You think of the test you did last Friday. Now your mind is racing, your heart is pounding, your mouth dries up, your hands feel cold and clammy, your forehead is pouring with sweat and your hands start trembling. As you imagine your teacher telling you that you can no longer stay in the class, the caveman inside you wants to come out. In situations like this you will often feel like running away but you may also feel like punching someone on the nose. Unfortunately you can't do either. Welcome to the modern world.

As your teacher ushers you into the class and closes the door, you're experiencing a full-blown episode of the fight or flight response. But since you can do neither, all of that energy is stuck inside you with no place to go. Your head feels like it's going to explode as your teacher begins to speak. 'Here it comes,' you think to yourself. But you're so shocked by what you hear you can't believe your ears. 'Sorry, I didn't quite understand you. Could you say that again?' you ask your teacher. 'Well done. Your test was excellent,' she repeats.

Our fight or flight response is designed to protect us from the sabre-tooth tigers that would have once hidden in the woods around us, threatening our physical survival. At times when our actual physical survival is threatened, there is no greater response to have on our side. When activated, the response causes a surge of adrenaline and other stress hormones to pump through our body, giving mothers the strength to lift cars off their trapped children and firemen the courage to run into blazing houses to save endangered victims.

When we face very real dangers to our physical survival it is invaluable. However, few of the 'tigers' we face in our day-to-day lives pose a serious physical threat to our existence. They aggravate us and cause us no end of stress, triggering the full activation of our fight or flight response. They make us become aggressive and hyper-vigilant, and tend to cause us to overreact to the situation in a counterproductive way. It is counterproductive to punch someone (the fight response) or run away (the flight response). This all leads to a difficult situation in which our automatic, predictable and unconscious reactions can actually work against our emotional, psychological and spiritual survival by causing a build-up of stress hormones.

By recognising the symptoms, we can begin to take steps to handle the stress overload. By learning to recognise the signals of fight or flight activation, we can avoid reacting excessively to events and fears that are not life threatening. In so doing, we use this extra energy to help us rather than harm us, borrowing the beneficial effects (heightened awareness, mental acuity and the ability to tolerate excess pain) in order to change our emotional environment and deal productively with our fears, thoughts and potential dangers.

(d) 🔊 Read the text again and listen. Which one of the following points does the article *not* raise?

1. In terms of our instincts, we are still very much like our cavemen ancestors.
2. The fight or flight response has enabled humans to perform some incredible physical actions.
3. The fight or flight response is an extremely useful resource to have in life-threatening situations.
4. Most of us very rarely find ourselves in extremely dangerous situations these days.
5. The fight or flight response has led psychologists to a number of fascinating insights into the brain.
6. It's not always possible to act out our fight or flight responses in modern life.
7. If we try to suppress our fight or flight response it can lead to a lot of stress.
8. If we can learn to recognise fight or flight responses in ourselves we can use them to our advantage.

3 Vocabulary

Feeling stressed

(a) Match the <u>underlined</u> words and expressions 1–7 from the text with the definitions a–g.

1	blood pressure <u>soars</u>	a	damp, the opposite of warm and dry
2	mind starts <u>racing</u>	b	gets higher really quickly
3	heart starts <u>pounding</u>	c	beats faster and louder
4	mouth <u>dries up</u>	d	the area above your eyes becomes wet
5	hands feel <u>clammy and cold</u>	e	feels too full to think properly
6	forehead starts <u>pouring with sweat</u>	f	thoughts move fast inside your head
7	head <u>feels like it's going to explode</u>	g	it becomes difficult to talk

(b) Work with a partner and write a sentence for each of the phrases in Exercise 3a.

When my mind starts racing I find it hard to concentrate on what I'm doing.

(c) We also experience many of these physical symptoms in other non-stressful situations. Make a list of some with your partner.

I sweat a lot when I have a hot shower / run too fast / drink a hot cup of tea.

My mind races when I get a good idea.

Discussion box

Work in pairs or small groups. Discuss these questions together.

1. Describe a situation where you have been faced with fight or flight.
2. How does it feel to relive the story? Have your emotions changed?

4 Grammar

Talking about tendencies

(a) Look at the examples from the text and answer the questions.

i *In situations like this you **will** often **feel like** running away.*

ii *They make us become aggressive and hyper-vigilant and **tend to cause us** to overreact to the situation in a counterproductive way.*

iii *The teacher's **always picking** on you.*

1 Does sentence *i* refer to the future or to no specific time?

2 Does sentence *ii* talk about something that is always true or often true?

3 Does sentence *iii* refer to an action happening at the moment of speaking or to no specific time at all?

(b) Complete the rule.

> **Rule:**
>
> There are a number of ways we can refer to actions that are often likely to happen. These include:
>
> - *always* + the .... tense: this usually refers to negative tendencies (but not always).
> - .... + infinitive: which in this case does not have a future reference, and refers to general tendencies.
> - .... *(not) to*: which refers to a person likely to behave in a certain way.

(c) Complete the text. Use one word for each gap.

If there's one thing I really don't like about school it's when my teacher asks me a question out of the blue. You know, when she suddenly calls out 'John, what do you think?' She usually does it when I'm trying to talk to Ben about football. My teacher's ¹ *always* complaining that I'm talking when I should be listening. Anyway, at times like this my mind tends ² .... go blank and I ³ .... inevitably forget everything that I've ever learned. It's extremely embarrassing. Unfortunately my teacher is always ⁴ .... this to me. I don't know why. The thing is that I tend ⁵ .... to mind answering questions when the teacher asks for a volunteer. In fact I ⁶ .... often be the first person with their hand in the air. The problem is that the teacher ⁷ .... not to choose me to answer these questions. Has she got something against me or am I paranoid?

(d) Do you sympathise with John or his teacher? Why / Why not?

(e) Work with a partner. Think of a situation when you felt you were being picked on. Take turns at giving each other advice.

5 Listen

(a) Work with a partner and answer these questions.

1 Imagine you are the student in the photo. How do you feel?

2 What advice would you give him?

3 Create a dialogue between the student and the person giving advice.

(b) 🔊 Listen to Keith talking about his stressful experiences. Tick (✓) the symptoms which are mentioned.

tiredness ☐
depression ☐
aching in his body ☐
panic attacks ☐
insomnia ☐
skin problems ☐
colds and flu ☐
headaches ☐
stomach problems ☐

(c) 🔊 Listen again and answer the questions.

1 How can a small amount of stress actually help you at exam time?

2 How had Keith managed his work at school?

3 Why did Keith think he was feeling so bad?

4 What advice did the doctor give Keith?

6 Vocabulary

Coping with stress

(a) Match the words 1–8 with words a–h to make expressions connected with stress.

1 take some
2 put
3 don't
4 take
5 don't be
6 chill
7 don't let
8 take a

a your feet up
b exercise
c things get on top of you
d break
e a deep breath
f overdo it
g out
h too hard on yourself

(b) Complete each sentence. Use an expression from Exercise 6a.

Less Stress

Get plenty of sleep
Whether you think you have time or not, always try to keep your sleep routine as regular as possible.
1 _____

Not sure whether you should stop or not? The answer is: do so. Taking short rests keeps you fresher for longer and you will learn more. Find the time to 2 _____ every now and then.

Time for yourself
Try to leave enough time in your revision schedule for some fun. You will need to put your books down and do something you enjoy for a while if you want to stay in a good mood.

Be realistic
3 _____ If you try to work too much each day, you won't take in the facts you're revising.

Eat properly
Make sure your diet includes plenty of fruit and veg. And remember if you're thirsty and can't decide whether to drink water or coffee then go for a glass of water every time. Caffeine causes more stress.

4 _____
It's a fantastic stress-buster. Go running, skateboarding, play a sport, or just take a walk around the block. You will feel more relaxed.

Be positive
5 _____ Your performance is influenced by whether your self-esteem is high or low. Make a quick list of five things you've done that you are proud of. This will put you in a good mood and you will learn more.

6 _____
If you are starting to lose it then it's time to relax and 7 _____ You need to:

- 8 _____
- tell yourself how well you are doing.
- remind yourself that everything is going to turn out all right.
- stand up straight and smile, you will feel a bit better straight away.

(c) Work with a partner and discuss your answers to Exercise 6b.

7 Speak

Work with a partner.

Student A: Look at the picture and imagine you are the person in it. Describe your situation to Student B.

Student B: Give your partner advice on how to deal with their problems. Then turn to page 123.

8 Speak and listen

(a) Work with a partner. Read the sentences and decide what the *it* refers to in each case.

1 Does it feel right?

   'It' could be referring to a relationship or trying on a shoe or item of clothing.

2 ... have to stare it in the eye.

3 ... once it's set its eyes on you.

4 I've got to face it.

5 If I don't make it someone else will

6 It's all around.

7 Can I take it?

(b) 🔊 Listen to the song and fill in the spaces with phrases from Exercise 8a.

(c) Read the expressions from Exercise 8a again. What do they mean in the context of the song?

Did you know ...?

Tori Amos, The Verve and Iron Maiden are just some of the varied musical influences for the Netherlands gothic-rock band Within Temptation. Robert Westerholt, a guitarist, and singer Sharon den Adel, his girlfriend, founded the band in 1996. The band have produced three albums to date, *Enter* (1997), *Mother Earth* (2000) and *The Silent Force* (2004). Tickets for their concerts in Europe, Canada and the USA sold out fast, thanks to their large number of fans.

Stand My Ground
by Within Temptation

I can see
when you stay low nothing happens
1 _____

Late at night
things I thought I put behind me
haunt my mind
I just know there's no escape
now 2 _____
but I won't run, 3 _____

[Chorus:]
Stand my ground, I won't give in
no more denying, 4 _____
won't close my eyes and hide the truth inside
5 _____
stand my ground

6 _____
getting stronger, coming closer
into my world
I can feel
that 7 _____
8 _____ ?
Though this might just be the ending
of the life I held so dear
but I won't run, there's no turning back from here

[Repeat chorus]

All I know for sure is I'm trying
I will always stand my ground
Stand my ground, I won't give in (I won't give in)
I won't give up (I won't give up)
no more denying, 9 _____
won't close my eyes and hide the truth inside
10 _____

28 Module 1

9 Write

Task

Imagine you are a student at a college. Write a report for the principal of your college on the reasons why students sometimes suffer from stress on their courses. Describe activities that tend to cause the most anxiety and the signs of pressure that students most commonly show. Also include a proposal on what the college could do to help students who suffer from stress.

1 Identify the two main sections of the writing task.

2 What is the aim of each of these sections?

3 What questions would you ask to get information for this report?

4 What information do you think you might find in each part of this task?

5 What kind of language do you think is appropriate in this kind of writing task?

(b) Look at the phrases below. Do you think they come from the report or the proposal?

1 Finally, we would like to explore other means of ...

2 We found that ...

3 Our research also looked into ...

4 As a consequence of our report, we have come up with a number of suggestions ...

5 88 per cent of those questioned identified this ...

6 We would recommend ...

7 Further investigation showed ...

8 Another suggestion would be ...

9 We would also advise ...

(c) Read the report and proposal and check your answers to Exercise 9b.

In a study of fifty college students we found that 72 per cent admitted to feeling some level of stress over the academic year. These levels ranged from 'feeling mildly stressed out on occasions' (45 per cent) to 'suffering from serious stress' (4 per cent). Further investigation showed that exams were clearly the time when most students felt under excess pressure. 88 per cent of those questioned identified this as the most stressful part of the school year. However, other causes of anxiety included homework and course work deadlines (52 per cent), difficult relationships with other students (18 per cent) and external problems (17 per cent). Our research also looked into the symptoms of stress that students most commonly showed. The most frequent was a 'feeling of panic'. This was felt by 67 per cent of students, although it must be said that this feeling varied in degrees of seriousness. Other symptoms that were mentioned included headaches (32 per cent), colds and feeling run down (23 per cent) and loss of sleep (22 per cent).

As a consequence of our report, we have come up with a number of suggestions that we feel the college could seriously consider implementing. Firstly we would recommend that this should be a problem that you actively encourage students to talk about and we would like to see a number of informal workshops on the subject. We would also advise that special after-school clinics should be set up for students to visit if they need to. Another suggestion would be to produce a college leaflet detailing things students can do to help themselves. Finally, we would like to explore other means of assessing students other than by exams.

We do realise that you have considerations of time and money but we also feel that if we can take steps to tackle this problem the benefits will be felt by both the student and the college.

(d) Choose one of the following tasks.

1 Write a report on students' lunchtime eating habits and make a proposal on how the school can cater for them better.

2 Write a report on students' favourite free time-activities and make a proposal on what new clubs the school could create.

For your portfolio

1 Grammar

a Put the verbs in brackets into the correct form of the past perfect.

1 When we got there, we saw that the town _had been destroyed_ by the tornado. (destroy)

2 By the time she arrived, I .... for more than an hour. (wait)

3 I had lots of money to spend on my holiday because I .... for months before I went. (save)

4 I was shocked when I saw that my bicycle .... (steal)

5 When the First World War came to an end, millions of soldiers .... (kill)

6 The teacher got angry when she realised that I .... to her. (not listen)

7 We were absolutely exhausted, because we .... since 6 in the morning. (work)

8 I hardly recognised the town – so many new houses .... since I left. (build)

☐ 7

b Circle the correct answer.

1 I .... phone you, but I forgot.
   a would   b was going to   c were going to

2 He called me to say he .... late.
   a would be   b was going to   c would

3 Steve and Alice .... help me out tonight.
   a were going to   b would   c would to

4 I'm sorry I didn't tell you before – I .... , but I never got the chance.
   a would   b was going to   c was going

5 I knew he .... come – he never does.
   a would   b was going to   c wouldn't

6 I .... buy a new computer, but in the end I decided to.
   a wouldn't   b was going to   c wasn't going to

7 They asked me if I .... help them on the project.
   a would   b was going   c would to

8 I'm sorry if I offended you – I thought you .... laugh at the joke.
   a was going to   b would   c weren't going to

☐ 7

c Put the words into the correct order.

1 a / I / green / bought / jacket / leather
   I bought a green leather jacket.

2 an / toy / old / it's / plastic ....

3 Japanese / a / it's / new / invention ....

4 a / shirt / it's / white / cheap / cotton
   ....

5 large / dining / round / they've / got / table / a
   ....

6 house / five-bedroomed / they / in / huge / live / a ....

7 drives / red / sports / car / Italian / a / he
   ....

8 high-heeled / beautiful / she's / shoes / black / wearing ....

☐ 7

d Rewrite each sentence with the adverb in brackets in the correct position. (There may be more than one possibility.)

1 John goes to visit his grandparents. (often)
   John often goes to visit his grandparents.

2 This is a good idea. (really)
   ....

3 It was a nice day for an excursion. (very)
   ....

4 Give that book back to me. (immediately)
   ....

5 We enjoyed the trip to Canterbury. (enormously)
   ....

6 I did not get the job. (unfortunately)
   ....

7 She looked at me. (in a curious way)
   ....

☐ 6

e Rewrite the sentences using the words in brackets.

1 He's often late. (tends) _He tends to be late._

2 My parents frequently complain about the music I play. (always) ....

3 Some people often go to the doctor with the smallest problem. (will) ....

4 He tells me what to do. (always) ....

5 Many teenagers don't eat healthy food. (tend)
   ....

6 My father's always telling the same old jokes! (will)
   ....

☐ 5

2 Vocabulary

(a) Complete each 'animal sound' word in the sentences. Make sure the word is in the correct form.

1 The little mice s _queaked_ when they saw the cheese.
2 My dog never bites, but he b_____ a lot.
3 When the snake began to h_____ , we thought it was going to attack.
4 My little sister loves seeing lambs and hearing them b_____ .
5 I asked him a question but he just g_____ like a pig!
6 It was hard to sleep in the tent – we thought we could hear a lion r_____ nearby.
7 We woke up when the cockerel in the farm started to c_____ .

	6

(b) Read each sentence and decide if the sentence that follows it is true or false.

1 I always prefer making informed decisions.
   I like to know some facts before I make my mind up. ✓
2 It was a snap decision.
   I thought about it for some time before I decided. ____
3 Let's mull things over for a while.
   We should think about it before deciding. ____
4 She always jumps to conclusions.
   She always makes quick but incorrect decisions. ____
5 I usually make my mind up quickly.
   I don't think about my decisions for a long time. ____
6 Dithering won't get us anywhere.
   It's a good idea for us to think about things for a long time. ____

	5

(c) Use the words in the box to complete the sentences.

> hoarding   jingle   slogan   logo   sandwich board
> ~~TV commercials~~

1 I don't like watching films on that channel – there are too many _TV commercials_ .
2 They've got a new magazine advertisement with the _____ : 'The bank that's made for you'.
3 We're designing a new _____ to put on the company's paper and bags.
4 The view from our flat has been ruined by an advertising _____ across the street.
5 I earned money in the summer by wearing a _____ , walking up and down the streets.
6 Their new _____ is really catchy – I find myself humming it all day!

	5

(d) Circle the correct option.

1 I'm tired – I'm going to (take) / make a break for ten minutes.
2 I was so scared, my heart began to pound / pour.
3 He knows he made a mistake, so don't be too hard / heavy on him.
4 He was trapped, and his mind started to run / race to find a way out.
5 You're exhausted! I think you've been overdoing / undoing things at work.
6 Go on, take a break! Put your feet / legs up for a few minutes.
7 I'm sure my blood pressure poured / soared during the exam today!
8 If you need to relax, close your eyes and take / make deep breaths.
9 Don't take everything so seriously! Chill / Cool out sometimes!
10 It's been a terrible day – everything really got on top of / on head of me.

	9

How did you do?

Tick (✓) a box for each section.

Total score:	😊	😐	☹️
57	Very good	OK	Not very good
Grammar	25 – 32	15 – 24	less than 15
Vocabulary	18 – 25	12 – 17	less than 12

Module 2
Fiction and reality

YOU WILL LEARN ABOUT ...

- Frank Abagnale, fake pilot and fraudster
- Women spies, World War II
- War and peace
- Inspiring buildings
- Metaphors we use and what they mean
- Virtual worlds on the Internet

 Can you match each picture with a topic?

YOU WILL LEARN HOW TO ...

Speak

- Talk about crime movies and why they are so popular
- Give a short talk based on a picture
- Talk about urban legends
- Tell a story or an anecdote
- Discuss what inspires your own creativity
- Talk about the positive and negative aspects of 'virtual worlds' on the Internet
- Talk about virtual holidays

Write

- A biography of a well-known person
- A newspaper story
- A poem using metaphors and similes
- An informal letter or email turning down an invitation

Read

- A true story of how good can prevail if someone is given a second chance
- An analysis of urban legends
- An article about 'Entropia', a virtual world on the internet
- Short pieces by famous people on what inspires their creativity

Listen

- A radio programme about two female spies during World War II
- A radio show called 'A likely story'
- A teenager's story of a trip to the USA with her family
- A linguist talking about the meaning of the metaphors we use in everyday life
- A report about multi-sensory virtual holidays

③

④

⑤

⑥

Use grammar

Can you match the names of the grammar points with the examples?

Reporting verb patterns

Deduction and probability

Causative *have* review

Modal passives

Cleft sentences

The exhibition **will be opened** by the Queen.

Have you ever **had a suit made** for you?

She **apologised for** having misled me.

What most inhabitants do first is find themselves a profession.

It sounds awful. You **must have been terrified**.

Use vocabulary

Can you think of two more examples for each topic?

War and peace	Expressions with *story*	Metaphors to describe emotions	Money
declare war	a likely story	make your blood boil	earn a living
peace negotiations	end of story	be on top of the world	purchase
....	....	....	....
....	....	....	....

(5) Double lives

* Reporting verb patterns review
* Vocabulary: crime
* Vocabulary: war and peace

1 Read and listen

(a) Read the text quickly. Which crime(s) did Frank Abagnale commit?

Behind the scenes
True stories from the movies

1 There are some people who felt that Steven Spielberg's film *Catch Me If You Can* was irresponsible, because it showed how a young man lived a life of thrills, adventure and glamour by cheating people out of their money. The film was based on the true story of a conman named Frank Abagnale, who during the late 1960s really did use his special 'talents' to lead an extraordinary life of crime. However, the real story of Frank Abagnale is not just how one teenager outsmarted the authorities for five years. It is also the story of how good can prevail if someone is given a second chance.

2 Frank's story begins when he was still a teenager. When he was 16, his parents separated, he didn't want to live with either of them, so he ran away to New York. Fortunately for him, he looked old for his age and once he had changed the 'four' on his driving licence to a 'three' he became ten years older. This was essential for his first scam, for which he needed a bank account. He made $40,000 from a scam that involved misleading other people into depositing money into his account instead of their own. By the time the bank found out what was going on, Frank had already taken the money and changed his identity.

3 Frank embarked on a life of deception which included forging a law diploma from Harvard, which he then used to get himself a job in a state attorney-general's office. He got a job at Georgia hospital by passing himself off as a doctor; and using a forged university degree, he spent a semester teaching sociology at Brigham Young University. He also managed to pass himself off as a stockbroker and, ironically, an FBI agent.

4 One of Frank's greatest desires was to see the world and this wish led to perhaps his most audacious act. For two years Abagnale pretended to be a Pan Am pilot, even though he didn't know anything about flying a plane. The first thing he needed was a uniform. He made a phone call to the company offices, told them what he wanted and they happily explained how to get one. Obtaining a fake ID was just as easy. With his ID and uniform, Abagnale would then introduce himself as a pilot at the check-in desk of an airline and secure jump-seats on flights all over the world. For the next few years Abagnale defrauded people all over the States and in twenty-six other countries. He had half the world's police forces looking for him, but he managed to give them the slip for many more months.

5 Abagnale was finally arrested in France after a flight attendant on an Air France plane recognised him from a wanted poster she had seen at an airport. Frank spent a total of five years in prison; first in Europe, and then in the US, where he confessed to having forged and cashed cheques to the value of $2.5 million using four different false identities. He was sentenced to 12 years for his crimes. However, in 1974 the government offered to release him from prison early in return for his help: he would work for free and help them understand how the typical conman operates. Frank agreed to assist them and from then on his life changed from master criminal to top crime-fighter.

6 Abagnale is the first to admit that what he did was wrong and he has apologised for having caused the authorities so much trouble. But he denies ever having intentionally caused harm to any individual. Of course, he realises that this is no excuse, which is why he was happy to lend his services to government agencies and financial institutions, helping them to protect themselves against the kind of crimes he once committed. He now has a company, Abagnale & Associates, which is one of the world's leading experts on forgery, embezzlement and other white-collar crimes. Furthermore, Frank has used the money he is making from his new source of income to pay back as many people that he cheated over the years as possible.

Frank's mission in life these days is finding ways of combating identity theft. He claims that this will be the crime of the future and that new technology is making it easier by the day.

(b) 🔊 Read the text again and listen. Answer the questions.

1 Why did Frank run away to New York?
2 Why did he change a number on his driving licence?
3 Frank pretended to have six different professions at different times. What were they?
4 Why did Frank pretend to be a pilot?
5 Was it easy for the police to catch Frank?
6 Why did the American government release him from prison early?

Discussion box

Work in pairs or small groups. Discuss these questions together.

1 Are films such as *Catch Me If You Can* irresponsible, because they portray successful crime?
2 If you could meet Frank Abagnale, what questions would you ask him?
3 Crime films are becoming increasingly popular with cinema-goers. Why do you think this is?

2 Vocabulary

Crime

(a) Match the words in the box from the text in Exercise 1 with definitions 1–9.

deception   fake   confess   defraud   forge   deny   mislead   ~~outsmart~~   give someone the slip

1   to obtain an advantage over someone by acting more cleverly and often by using a trick. *outsmart*
2   to cause someone to believe something that is not true
3   when people hide the truth, especially to get an advantage
4   not real, but made to look or seem real
5   to escape from someone
6   to admit that you have done something wrong
7   to say that something is not true
8   to take something illegally from a person or company, or to prevent someone from having something that is legally theirs by deceiving them
9   to make an illegal copy of something in order to deceive

(b) Match the two parts of the sentences.

1   Once I forged my mum's   a   but she managed to give them the slip.
2   You can buy really cheap fake   b   the facts.
3   Only a fool would deny   c   out of their savings.
4   He misled hundreds of people into   d   as he'd invented some details on his CV.
5   She could easily pass herself off   e   she had cheated in the exam.
6   Every police car in the area was on the lookout for her,   f   you need to outsmart the other contestants.
7   He defrauded them   g   signature to get out of school early.
8   He admitted to getting the job by deception,   h   as my sister.
9   If you want to win the competition,   i   paying into a non-existent retirement fund.
10 She confessed that   j   designer sunglasses in the market.

3 Grammar

Reporting verb patterns review

(a) Rewrite the sentences using the reporting verb in brackets.

1   'Do you want to live with your father or your mother?' (ask)
   The judge asked if I wanted to live with my father or my mother.
2   'I forged paychecks to the value of $2.5 million.' (confess to)
   He _____
3   'We'll release you from prison early if you help us understand how conmen work.' (offer)
   The government _____
4   'What I did was wrong.' (admit)
   Abagnale _____
5   'I'm sorry that I caused so much trouble to the authorities.' (apologise)
   He _____
6   'I certainly didn't intend to cause harm to any individual.' (deny)
   He _____
7   'Identity theft is the crime of the future.' (claim)
   Frank _____
8   'People should take this threat very seriously.' (advise)
   He _____

(b) Answer the questions about the sentences in Exercise 3a.

1   What pattern follows the verbs *claim / admit*?
2   What pattern follows the verbs *apologise for / deny / confess to*?
3   After *apologise for*, *deny* and *confess to*, how do we know that the other action is in the past?

c Match sentences 1–6 with reporting verbs a–f.

1 'I'm sorry that I misled you,' she said.
2 'Yes, it's true – the thief outsmarted me,' the policeman said.
3 'Did you forge the document?' he said.
4 'It's very easy to deceive people,' he said.
5 'It was me who defrauded the company,' she said.
6 'I did not pass myself off as a lawyer,' he said.

a deny
b ask
c admit
d confess
e apologise
f claim

d Rewrite the sentences in Exercise 3c using the reporting verbs.

She apologised for having misled me.

4 Read

a Read the text quickly. Choose a title 1–3 that you think fits best.

1 How to be a spy
2 Women secret agents
3 Living a double life

Webpedia the online encyclopedia

Great Britain declared war on Germany in 1939 after Germany had invaded several European countries, and the following year the British set up the Special Operations Executive (SOE). This was an organisation of secret agents: people who did not fight in battles, but who went to help local resistance movements in places occupied by the enemy.

The SOE recruited its agents from a wide range of backgrounds. Often the lives of ordinary civilians were utterly transformed when they were thrown into the dangerous world of espionage. Many of the agents were young women, chosen because they had one vital skill: the ability to speak a European language like a native. They were given false identities to protect themselves once they had left Britain, and they were trained in marksmanship, using explosives, the transmission of coded messages, survival in the wilderness, and how to resist interrogation. In short, they learned everything necessary to live a double life behind enemy lines. But it was a dangerous job and there were many casualties amongst the agents.

SOE agents played an invaluable role right up to 1945, when Germany surrendered and a peace treaty was signed.

b Answer the questions.

1 Why did Britain declare war on Germany?
2 Who did the SOE secret agents go to help?
3 Where did the agents work?
4 What kind of people did SOE persuade to join them?
5 What special ability did many of the recruits have?
6 What five things did they have to learn about before they started work?

c Work with a partner. What do you imagine the life of a spy is like? Give examples of any real-life spies you know about.

5 Vocabulary

War and peace

Check the text in Exercise 4a for the meanings of the words and expressions in the box. Complete the text with the words in the box.

> declared war   ~~invaded~~
> surrendered   signed
> recruited   casualties
> battles   peace negotiations
> fought

Freedonia and Sylvania lived together peacefully for many years. But then Freedonia [1] *invaded* Sylvania, and as a consequence Sylvania [2] .... on Freedonia. Sylvania did not have enough soldiers so they [3] .... new ones to go and fight in the [4] .... The two [5] .... for many years. Despite the heavy [6] .... , neither side [7] .... Finally, after five years of war, [8] .... began and they [9] .... a treaty.

6 Listen

a 🔊 Listen to the radio programme about two women, Lilian Rolfe and Odette Hallowes who worked for the SOE in France in World War II. Tick (✓) the correct boxes in the table. (Some information is true of both women.)

Who ...	Lilian	Odette
1 was born in France?		
2 did not originally intend to work for the SOE?		
3 worked as a radio operator?		
4 entered France by air?		
5 went by the name of Lise?		
6 was captured and tortured?		
7 has a street named after her?		
8 survived the war?		

b 🔊 Listen again. Mark the statements *T* (true) or *F* (false). Correct the false statements.

1 Lilian Rolfe went to London to join the Women's Army. ☐
2 Lilian arrived in France by parachute and carrying a large radio with her. ☐
3 Lilian's job was to maintain the deliveries of arms to the French Resistance. ☐
4 Lilian was interrogated for eight months and gave the enemy some important information. ☐
5 Odette delivered messages in France and found houses where she could use her radio. ☐
6 When Odette and the officer arrived at the prison, they put a plan together. ☐
7 During her interrogation, Odette shared a prison cell with Lilian Rolfe. ☐
8 When Odette escaped, she forced a German officer to take her to the French Resistance. ☐

c Imagine you are either Lilian or Odette. Write a page in your diary.

7 Speak

①

②

③

④

a Look at the photos and compare them. Which one would you choose to define peace? Why?

b Work with a partner. Choose one of the pictures and prepare to talk about it for 1–2 minutes. Then swap roles and choose a different picture. Think about:

- what is in the picture and what it makes you think of.
- whether you like or dislike it and give reasons why.
- using expressions such as: I think that this is the best because ... / What do you think about this picture here?

Literature in mind

8 Read

a Read extract 1 quickly. What do we know about Flight Lieutenant Gregory from the letter?

Dear Miss Gray,

Further to our telephone conversation today I am writing to confirm that while we have received no news of Flt Lt Gregory since he left on a mission some time ago, we have no reason to believe the worst. Although we are a standard RAF squadron independent of other organisations, albeit working in liaison with other services, you will no doubt appreciate that I am not at liberty to disclose details of the flight, either with regard to its destination or in respect of its operational purpose. I can tell you that Flt Lt Gregory is an extremely able pilot and a patriotic officer with a proper sense of duty. My own belief is that for any one of a number of possible operational reasons he was unable to execute the full purpose of his mission but that he will make every endeavour to contact us when it is safe and prudent for him to do so. He will be officially posted 'Missing' but I'm sure you have every faith in him, as most assuredly do his colleagues.

Yours sincerely,

Allan Wetherby, Squadron Leader

b Read extract 2. Circle the correct answers a, b or c.

1 Wetherby thinks that Gregory has gone missing because:
   a he didn't have enough petrol to complete the journey
   b the agent he had arranged to meet did not arrive
   c his French was not good enough for him to survive

2 Charlotte dedicated herself to completing her training because:
   a she wanted to get perfect results in her exams
   b she promised Marigold that she would
   c she wanted to find Gregory

3 Charlotte and Marigold's roommate Liliane:
   a was training to be a typist
   b had invented a cover story where she was a typist
   c thought she was training to be a typist

4 They needed to have a cover story in case:
   a they were interrogated
   b a train was derailed
   c they were asked to become actors

2

On the telephone, Wetherby had told her 'strictly between ourselves' that the most likely explanation was that the man Gregory was supposed to pick up had not been there. Without the agent or the support of his network, Gregory would have been unable to refuel and therefore obliged to 'make his own arrangements'. Charlotte pictured him begging petrol from a farmer in his dreadful French and finding himself reported to the Vichy authorities; she tried to develop this picture in her mind because the only alternative was to believe that he was already dead.

She told Marigold nothing of her worries as the train headed out into Surrey. She had confided in Daisy, and that was enough. Now she would complete her training with the greatest assiduity, and when it was finished she would go to France and find him.

Security, recognition, interrogation and security. That, the intelligence officer running the course told them with a smirk at his witty repetition, was what Group D was all about. Charlotte and Marigold were among only six women on the course; they sat next to each other and learned to identify every German plane and badge and rank and regiment. Vaguer but more important were the instructions for recognising German counter-intelligence officers, the Abwehr and their colleagues, of whom there were unknown numbers in France – presumed standing at station ticket barriers, sitting in cafés, idly making bogus calls from public telephone boxes. In her state of stunned concentration Charlotte committed every detail to memory and entered mistake-free test papers when required.

A grave, actorish man in his sixties gave them practical hints on looking ordinary and natural. It was no use knowing a cover story and giving away nothing under interrogation, he told them, they had to look at all times like people who didn't even have a cover story.

Charlotte shared a bedroom with Marigold and a young woman called Liliane, whose mother was French. She took the course more lightly than the other two, and claimed that when she first went to Scotland it was in answer to an advertisement for bilingual secretaries; the first time she realised she was not being groomed to be a typist was when they offered to instruct her in silent killing.

The three of them were joined by three men for an exercise in interrogation. They were told to prepare a cover story giving details not only of assumed identities but of the precise way in which they had all passed the four hours of the previous afternoon, in the course of which a local train had been derailed. Each was then to be interrogated separately.

(c) Match the words 1–8 from the text with the words a–h of similar meaning.

1 likely (paragraph 1)
2 assiduity (paragraph 2)
3 smirk (paragraph 3)
4 witty (paragraph 3)
5 bogus (paragraph 3)
6 stunned (paragraph 3)
7 grave (paragraph 4)
8 in the course of (paragraph 6)

a during
b probable
c false
d dedication
e very shocked and surprised
f unpleasant smile
g funny in a clever way
h serious and solemn

(d) 'She had confided in Daisy'. Work in pairs to create a dialogue between Charlotte and Daisy, where Charlotte tells Daisy her fears about Gregory and her plans to find him. Use expressions from Exercise 8c where possible.

9 Write

(a) Read the biography of Sebastian Faulks, the author of *Charlotte Gray*, and underline the important information. Think about the following points to help you.

- his major achievements
- main themes of his books
- his most popular books
- his family history
- prizes won

Sebastian Faulks was born in 1953, the son of a judge and an actress, and grew up in Newbury. He studied at Wellington College and Emmanuel College, Cambridge, but claims he didn't enjoy his time at either of them because they were male-dominated with very few female students. He was the first literary editor of the *Independent* and became deputy editor of the *Independent on Sunday* before leaving in 1991 to concentrate on writing. He has been a columnist for the *Guardian* (1992–8) and the *Evening Standard* (1997–9) and he still enjoys contributing articles and reviews to a number of newspapers and magazines. His first novel, *A Trick of the Light*, was published in 1984. His other novels include *The Girl at the Lion d'Or* (1989), set in France between the First and Second World Wars, and the best-selling *Birdsong* (1993), the story of a young Englishman called Stephen Wraysford and his harrowing experiences fighting in northern France during the First World War. His fifth novel, *Charlotte Gray* (1998), completes the loose trilogy of books about France with an account of the adventures of a young Scottish woman who becomes involved with the French Resistance during the Second World War. A film adaptation of the novel, starring Cate Blanchett, was first screened in 2002. Most of his novels have a war theme, along with an element of romance. One of his most acclaimed books is the non-fiction *The Fatal Englishman: Three Short Lives*, a biography of artist Christopher Wood, airman Richard Hillary, and spy Jeremy Wolfenden.

Sebastian Faulks lives with his wife and family in London. He was awarded the CBE in 2002.

(b) Read the notes about the ex-Secretary-General of the UN and humanitarian, Kofi Annan. Use the information to write a biography about him.

- Kofi Annan, born in 1938, in Ghana
- name means 'born on Friday', has a twin sister
- family part of Ghanaian elite, grandparents and uncles are tribal chiefs
- studied economics at university
- speaks English, French and many African languages
- first job in 1962 with WHO
- was head of Ghana Tourist Board from 1974 to 1976
- since 1977 been working for the UN
- was made Secretary-General of the UN in 1997, retired in December 2006

For your portfolio

Legend or truth?

✱ Deduction and probability
✱ Vocabulary: expressions with story

1 Read and listen

(a) Each picture shows part of a story. What do you think is happening in each one?

(b) Read the text quickly to check your ideas.

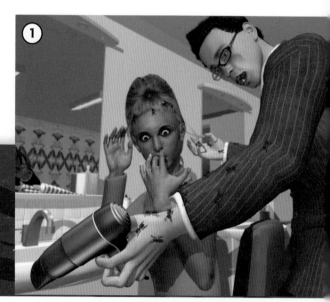

The rise and rise of urban legends

So there's this woman who spent lots of money on a special hairdo and then refused to wash it for months because she didn't want to lose the style. After a while, her head started to itch, so she went back to get it done again. When the hairdresser let her hair down, they found a nest of ants living in it. You don't believe it? OK, try this one. A friend of a friend of mine, at university, bought an essay on the Internet. Unfortunately for her, it had been written 15 years earlier by the person who was now her tutor. The tutor recognised it, but gave her an A anyway and told her that his teacher at the time had failed it, but he'd always thought it was worth an A.

You could have heard one, if not both, of these stories before. They are both classic examples of urban legends, and stories like these have become such an integral part of modern life that A _____ . But just in case you have somehow managed to miss them, let me quickly fill you in.

Urban legends, or urban myths as they're commonly known in the UK, are stories that are quickly passed on by word of mouth or by email. They can be about anything and everything, although certain topics will often crop up: some favourites are crime and horror, schools and universities, cases of food contamination and the Internet. These stories, often incredible, horrific or funny, are always told as if they are true and usually happened to 'a friend of a friend'. However, although occasionally they may really have happened, they will usually have been entirely made up. Perhaps the best definition of an urban legend is that B _____ .

People started using the term 'urban legend' more than seventy years ago, but it was only in the 1990s that C _____ . Many experts point to the 'organ donor' story as the grandfather of the modern legends. You must have come across the story of a stranger in town

c 🔊 Read the text again and listen. Fill in the spaces A–F in the text with phrases 1–7. There is one clause you do not need to use.

1 the term really came into use
2 academics now discuss the wider implications of these contemporary legends
3 you can always tell whether a story is true or not
4 there can't be anyone left who doesn't know what they are
5 we are so ready to believe that a story might be true
6 they have never been more popular
7 it's a story that's too good to be true

who wakes up to find himself in a bath of ice and with one of his kidneys removed. It can be traced back to Los Angeles sometime in 1994, when it spread panic throughout the area and even led to the local police issuing warnings to people visiting the town. Of course, a real case like this has never been recorded.

These days the spread of the Internet has given urban legend tellers an immediate audience of millions, and ᴰ_____ . There are now even websites dedicated to investigating the truth behind the thousands of urban legends circulating in cyberspace. Is it true that a university library is sinking because the architect forgot to calculate the weight of the books into his design? Do American university students really get an automatic A+ in their final exams if their roommate commits suicide? You can find the answers to these and other questions on the Internet.

These stories have become such a part of our everyday life that ᴱ_____ . Ever since it was founded at the University of Sheffield in 1982, the International Society for Contemporary Legend Research has held an annual conference in North America or Europe to discuss the latest stories and their significance. Over the years, these meetings have looked at a wide range of issues – from mankind's compulsion for storytelling to the cautionary nature of many of the legends; from why it is that we get so much pleasure from passing on such stories to a comparison between urban legends and traditional fairy-tales.

Recently, many academics have shown more interest in what current urban legends tell us about modern society and particularly how they reflect the climate of fear in which many of us live. Experts argue that whether or not the stories are true is largely irrelevant. What is interesting is that ᶠ_____ and, in some cases, we will change our behaviour because of it. As an example, the following legend is often quoted: an initiation ceremony for many American gangs involves driving your car at night with no lights on, and when you come across a car that flashes you to advise you of your mistake, you must turn your car around and chase the other car until you force it to crash. Now, although not one single case of this has ever been reported, a lot of people now won't flash their lights at other cars through fear that this could happen to them.

d Read the text again and answer the questions.

1 What examples are given of things that urban legends are often about?
2 According to the article, are most urban legends true or untrue?
3 What is believed to be the first 'urban legend' and what effect did it have at the time?
4 What can you do on the Internet with regard to urban legends?
5 Four examples are given of things the academic conferences discuss. What are they?
6 What do experts think is more important than whether the legends are true or not?

e Find words or phrases in the text with these meanings.

1 very good instances (paragraph 2)
   classic examples
2 through people talking to each other (paragraph 3)
3 appear (paragraph 3)
4 resulted in (paragraph 4)
5 a lot of different topics (paragraph 6)
6 a time/situation when most people feel afraid (paragraph 7)
7 generally not very important (paragraph 7)
8 no examples at all (paragraph 7)

Discussion box

Work in pairs or small groups. Discuss these questions together.

1 Which is your favourite and your least favourite of the urban legends in the text?
2 Have you heard or read any urban legends recently?
3 Do you agree that urban legends 'reflect the climate of fear in which many of us live'?

2 Grammar

Deduction and probability

(a) Read the sentences and (circle) the correct answer.

1 There **can't be** anyone who doesn't know them.
   a it is not possible   b it is possible
   c it is not certain

2 People **might believe** a story.
   a it is certain   b it is possible
   c it is not possible

3 Certain topics **will crop up**.
   a it is not probable   b it is possible
   c it is very probable

4 They **may** really **have happened**.
   a it is very probable   b it is not possible
   c it is certain

5 You **must have come across** this story.
   a it is not certain   b it is certain
   c it is not possible

6 The stories **will** usually **have been made up**.
   a it is possible   b it is not certain
   c it is not possible

(b) Discuss the differences between these pairs of sentences.

1 a There's someone at the door. It must be James.
   b There's someone at the door. It might be James.

2 a Ask Monica where her brother is – she'll know.
   b Ask Monica where her brother is – she must know.

3 a It's seven o'clock now. My sister will have arrived in New York.
   b It's seven o'clock now. My sister must have arrived in New York.

(c) Complete the sentences with a modal verb plus the verb in brackets. There may be more than one answer.

1 I'm not sure where Natasha is, but she *..might be..* outside in the garden.

2 Pete's got a foreign accent, so he .... (not be) from this country.

3 Let's ask Fred about the homework – he .... (know) how to do it.

4 It's a pretty unbelievable story! Jose .... (make) it up.

5 Alana hung up in the middle of our conversation. I .... (say) something she didn't like.

6 Peter and Thomas know everything about horror films, so they .... (watch) thousands of them.

(d) Work with a partner and compare your answers to Exercise 2c. Where there are differences, discuss the difference in meanings between your answers.

3 Listen

(a) Look at the pictures of the two stories. What do you think is happening in each story?

Story 1

a

b

c

Story 2 d

e

f

(b) 🔊 Listen to a radio show called *A Likely Story*. Number the pictures in Exercise 3a in the order you hear the information. Write *T* (true) or *F* (false) to say if the story is true or not.

(c) Work with a partner and use the pictures to retell each of the two stories.

4 Vocabulary

Expressions with story

a Match the expressions 1–8 with their definitions a–h.

1 to cut a long story short
2 a sob story
3 end of story
4 it's the same old story
5 that's a likely story
6 it's the story of my life
7 his or her side of the story
8 make up a story

a an excuse/explanation that's very hard to believe
b something (unwanted) that frequently happens to you
c the events as he or she describes them
d a story someone tells you to make you feel sorry for them
e all that needs to be said about something
f to tell the main facts, not the details
g to invent an excuse
h something negative that has happened to you many times before

b Read the dialogues and (circle) the correct words.

1 A: Dad – I thought I might go out with my friends tonight.
    B: Well, OK, but if you want to go out, you have to do your homework first – *end of story / a sob story*!

2 A: Where's your homework?
    B: Sorry, miss, I had to go shopping and cook dinner and … well, *to cut a long story short / to make up a story*, I didn't have time to do it.

3 A: I'm sorry I lost your camera, but really it was Sally's fault.
    B: Well, I'm going to talk to Sally and hear *the story of her life / her side of the story*.

4 A: Let's go to the cinema.
    B: Yeah, good idea – but I'm broke, can you buy my ticket?
    A: Again?! *It's the same old story / End of story*, isn't it?

5 A: Sorry I didn't come last night!
    B: But why didn't you phone me? And please don't *make up a story / cut a long story short* about your phone not working!

6 A: Where's your homework?
    B: Well, I did it, but then my dog ate it.
    A: Oh, right! That's *a likely story / a sob story*!

7 A: Here's your test. You got 20 per cent. You failed!
    B: Again? *It's the story of my life / It's my side of the story*!

8 A: Has Mike given you back the money you lent him?
    B: Not yet. He *told me a sob story / cut a long story short* about how he had to spend a lot of money to go and visit his sick grandmother.

c 🔊 Listen and check. Work with a partner and practise the dialogues in Exercise 4b.

5 Speak

Play *A Likely Story*. Work in pairs, Student A and Student B. Student B: turn to page 123.

Student A:
Here is the outline of an urban legend. You have five minutes to think of more details for it and make it as convincing as possible. Then you must tell Student B the story. Student B has to decide if it is true or not.

This happened in California.
A couple were driving their car and their baby was in the car.
They stopped for a break. They also took the baby out of the car.
They forgot to put the baby back in the car and drove off.
Two hours later they found the baby again and it was OK.

Speaking

6 Listen and speak

a Work with a partner. Look at pictures a–f quickly and say what they show.

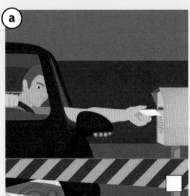 **a**

 **b**

 **c**

 **d**

 **e**

 **f**

b 🔊 Listen to Karen's story about her trip to the USA with her family. Write the numbers 1–6 in the boxes in Exercise 6a in the correct order of the story.

c 🔊 Listen again. Number the boxes in the order Karen says the phrases in.

- ☐ all of a sudden
- ☐ off we went
- ☐ lying on the ground were
- ☐ the machine kind of ate the ticket
- ☐ he pressed them again and again and again
- ☐ would you believe it
- ☐ that was the amazing thing

d Work with a partner. Discuss how the other phrases in Exercise 6c make the story more dramatic.

e Think of a story that you have experienced or that you have heard. It could be:

- something that happened at school
- something that happened on holiday
- something that happened at home
- something that happened when you were in town

Work in small groups. Tell each other your story.
Note how often each person uses dramatic storytelling devices.
Vote on who told the most interesting story.

7 Pronunciation

Stress in phrases

🔊 Turn to page 122.

8 Write

a) Read the newspaper article. Do you believe the story? What kind of newspaper do you think it comes from?

Doctors at San Antonio Community hospital were able last night to save the life of 17-year-old George Brooke from a mysterious illness that had ¹*dramatically / miraculously / tragically* already claimed the lives of his father and grandfather years before. But as well as preventing the young man from dying, medical experts have also managed to solve an age old mystery that has been haunting the Texan family for generations.

Mr Brooke became ill late on Tuesday night. When his mother Barbara saw the symptoms, she immediately feared the worst. His skin turned grey and he began to have problems breathing. It seemed she was watching exactly the same illness that had taken her husband 20 years earlier and her father-in-law 20 years before that. The boy was rushed to hospital where doctors diagnosed him as suffering from the effects of snake venom. Although the poisoning was already in the later dangerous stages of development, they were ²*miraculously / luckily / tragically* able to administer the antidote in time.

However, the doctors were still left mystified as to how the venom had entered the body. They found no snake bites on his body and the boy hadn't reported seeing a snake that day. The only thing he could remember that was a little strange was feeling a small prick on his foot when he had put on his pair of cowboy boots. It turned out that it had been George's birthday that day and one of his presents had been a pair of boots that had originally belonged to his grandfather. When questioned further Barbara told of how both other members of the family had died ³*overwhelmingly / mysteriously / in unexplained circumstances* while wearing these boots. There was talk of how the boots had been cursed by a

rattlesnake that her father-in-law had stamped to death while wearing the boots a few days before he died. She had always refused to believe this story. The doctors examined the boots and, ⁴*in a spectacular turn of events / incredibly / mysteriously*, found the fang of a rattlesnake embedded in the sole of the right boot. ⁵*Incredibly / Finally / Amazingly* it still contained enough poison to kill several people. ⁶*At last / Finally / Astonishingly*, it seems that the revenge of the snake is over.

b) Read the story again. Which of the three adverbs does **not** fit each of the spaces?

c) What type of story do you expect from each of these titles?

1 Killer snake strikes from beyond the grave.
2 Family mystery finally solved.
3 These boots were made for killing.
4 Teenage survives deadly snake bite.

d) Look again at the two stories in Exercise 3 on page 42. Choose one of them and write it as a newspaper article. Use the story above as a model. Alternatively – create your own urban myth!

7 Inspiration and creation

* Causative *have* review
* Modal passives (present and past)
* Vocabulary: metaphors to describe emotions

1 Read and listen

a Work with a partner. Make a list of ten things that could inspire writers, singers and dancers.

What inspires the inspirational?

Where does creativity come from? How do we find our best ideas, our greatest expressions of intellect and imagination? What goes on in our minds is as individual as we are – yet it has the power to define our lives and change the world. From artists and authors to campaigners and politicians, we ask: What's your inspiration? This week, we ask the question to three artists.

Darcey Bussell, Prima ballerina

Benjamin Zephaniah, Poet

Joan Armatrading, Singer and songwriter

I am inspired mainly by bright colours and beautiful views. When you live in a big city with long winters, I think you need them to revive your enthusiasm for life. I've always painted my walls vivid colours, like bright pink. In my first flat, I had a bathroom that was painted purple. It made everybody go 'Woooh!'

My mother was into colours and loved to mix them. I particularly love red and pink together, although the combination can appal some people. I love to dress my two daughters in vibrant colours. I don't wear enough colour myself, though. I once had a wonderful costume made for me that was red chiffon with wonderful Indian trousers. It was for the part of Nikiya in La Bayadère.

What motivated me to start thinking politically and putting my poetry into words was the image of a starving child in the Biafran war. We were watching the news on TV and I remember asking my mother why that baby looked like that – the thin arms, the swollen belly. My mother explained that the child was starving largely because there was fighting going on. And I was just becoming aware of racism and I said: 'Why do white people do this to us all the time?', and my mother said: 'No, this is black people hurting each other.' I couldn't believe how horrible it was. I thought I wanted to do something. I felt these were children like me. They should be outside with me, playing football.

Later on in life, I remember being told that working-class black people like me should get an apprenticeship, work, find a nice dark-skinned girl and have children. I remember thinking: if that's it, if that's all there is for me, then I'm going to kill myself. And then I remembered the Biafran kid and the image drove me to live to help others live. From then on, I knew what to do with my poetry and my life. And I'm very grateful for that image.

Everyday conversations can be an incredible source of inspiration. A person could say something trivial, just a word or a phrase, and it can become a song.

The other day, somebody was telling me that their building was set on fire. So it was arson; something called a glory fire. I hadn't ever heard that phrase, but it's used to describe what happens when somebody deliberately starts a fire in order to put it out and claim the praise.

Anyway, it had gone horribly wrong and there was a really serious fire. I was shown pictures of the building. But I immediately wrote down the term, and all these things were coming into my head; I was playing with associations, thinking how a glory fire could be used to refer to something else. Things like that spur me on immediately into putting down ideas for songs. Whether that song gets written – well, you'll have to wait and see when the next album comes out.

b What do you know about any of the people in the photos? Where do you think they get their inspiration from? Read the text quickly to find the answers.

c 🔊 Read the text again and listen. Answer the questions.

1   How do bright and beautiful things help Darcey with big city life?
2   What reaction do some people have to red and pink together according to Darcey?
3   Why was Benjamin moved by the photos of people he saw on TV from the Biafran war?
4   How did Benjamin feel about the expectation for working-class black people?
5   How does Joan create her song lyrics?

d Which person in Exercise 1a refers to the following ideas:

1   the frustration of being stereotyped.
2   the emotional effect colours can have on people.
3   how inspiration can come from everyday conversations.
4   the emotional impact a visual memory can have on finding meaning in life.

e Find the words in the text and choose the correct definition.

1	appal	make someone feel strong feelings of disapproval / interest or attract someone
2	vivid	showing a desire to hurt someone / very brightly coloured
3	deliberately	pleasantly soft or light; not strong / done on purpose
4	arson	the crime of intentionally starting a fire / a person who intentionally starts a fire
5	refer to	write about something / show the connection between two or more things
6	spur on	secretly gather and report information / make an activity happen faster

Discussion box

Work in pairs or small groups. Discuss these questions together.

1   Where do you get your inspiration from?
2   How important is visual inspiration for you? What kinds of images do you regard most inspirational?
3   Are there any specific songs or pieces of music that inspire your creativity? Why / Why not?

2 Grammar

Causative *have* review

a Look at the sentence from the text about Darcey Bussell and answer the question.

I once had a wonderful costume made for me that was red chiffon with wonderful Indian trousers.

In this sentence, who made the costume?

b Complete the rule using the example in Exercise 2a.

Rule:

● This structure is formed with the verb *to* .... + object + the .... of the main verb.

We can use this structure for things that we intend to happen. We ask or pay someone to do these things for us as a service.

c Complete each sentence using the *have something done* structure.

1   I went to the hairdresser last week and I *had my hair cut* (my hair / cut)
2   She hired a painter and she .... (her house / paint)
3   Paul went to a tailor and he .... (a suit / make)
4   It was a great weekend because I .... (my letter / publish) in my favourite magazine.
5   While my friends were on holiday, they .... (their cat / look after) by their neighbours.
6   I've had lots of headaches recently. I think I should .... (my blood pressure / check)

3 Listen

a Work with a partner. Look at the pictures and try to work out each metaphor 1–4.

①

②

③

④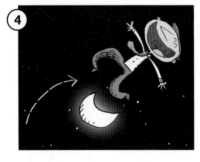

b 🔊 Listen to the interview and check your ideas from Exercise 4a. What do each of the metaphors mean?

c 🔊 Listen again and (circle) the correct answers.

1 Why does Jane love metaphors?
   a Because they let us experiment with our language.
   b Because they help us understand grammatical rules.
   c Because they allow us to invent new words.

2 Which of the following is not a feature of a metaphor?
   a They don't mean exactly what they say.
   b They involve a comparison.
   c They are mainly used in spoken language.

3 What does she use the example 'I feel like I'm frying fish at three o'clock in the morning' to say?
   a Anyone can make up a metaphor.
   b Metaphors only really work if we can see a connection between the things being compared.
   c A good metaphor comes from the imagination.

4 According to Jane, how often does a person use a metaphor in spoken language?
   a Every 10 seconds.
   b Every 15 seconds.
   c Every 30 seconds.

5 Why is Jane interested in the metaphors that we make up ourselves?
   a Because they can help us understand the person better.
   b Because they are usually more creative.
   c Because they tell us interesting things about our language.

4 Vocabulary

Metaphors to describe emotions

a Complete the sentences with the words in the box. Use a dictionary if you need to.

> happy   nervous   embarrassed
> shocked   angry   frustrated   mad
> depressed   disappointed   calm

a If you *feel like you're banging your head against a brick wall*, then you feel _____ .

b If you have *butterflies in your stomach*, you feel _____ .

c If you tell someone *you're on top of the world*, you feel _____ .

d If you're *feeling a bit down in the dumps*, you feel _____ .

e If something *makes your blood boil*, you are _____ .

f If someone *has got a screw loose*, they are a bit _____ .

g If you *don't know where to put yourself*, you're _____ .

h If you *don't know what has hit you*, you are _____ .

i If you're *really cut up* about something, you're _____ .

j If you tell someone to *keep their hair on*, you want them to keep _____ .

b Complete the sentences using expressions from Exercise 4a.

1 She says and does the strangest things! Sometimes I think she's *got a screw loose* .

2 I was so nervous before the exam! I had _____ .

3 I accidentally dropped ice cream on her brand new dress! It was awful! I didn't _____ .

4 James got dumped by Jenny, and he's _____ about it.

5 I don't really want to talk now. I'm feeling _____ – but I'll be better tomorrow.

6 That man's always so rude to me! It really _____ .

7 I talk to him, but he just doesn't listen. I feel like _____ .

8 _____ ! We need to keep calm and think of how we can deal with this problem.

c Work with a partner and create a story in response to the questions. Make notes and then tell your story to another pair of students. Do not write the story.

- Think of a person: Who is it? How old? Where from? Job? Personality?
- One day they were a feeling a bit down in the dumps. Why?
- In order to feel on top of the world again, they went on a journey. Where to?
- There they became friends with someone who people said had got a screw loose. What was that person like?
- On the last day before returning home, they discovered something that made their blood boil. What was it? How did they react? How did the story end?

5 Grammar
Modal passives (present and past)

a Read the sentences from the text. Complete the sentences with the words in the box.

> scared   used   accused of   made

1 If we do, we **might be** _____ not speaking the language properly.
2 A good metaphor is a great example of how language **should be** _____ .
3 She **must have been** really _____ by the idea.
4 A connection **can be** _____ between the things that we are comparing.

b Which sentence in Exercise 5a refers to a past situation?

c Use the sentences in Exercise 5a to complete the rule.

> **Rule:**
> - We can use modals in the passive voice by using the modal verb + _____ (present) or _____ (past), and the past participle of the main verb.

d Write the sentences using the passive. Do not use the words *someone* or *people*.

1 (Someone) might break the record soon.
   The record might be broken soon.
2 (People) can send applications by email.
   _____
3 (Someone) must win the prize.
   _____
4 (People) will not forget his name.
   _____
5 (People) should put these things back.
   _____
6 (Someone) might have stolen your purse.
   _____
7 (Someone) must have opened this door.
   _____
8 (Someone) should have invited her to the party.
   _____

e Complete the text with a word from the box.

> be   been   would   will   passed
> can't   have

Paula knew she should [1]_____ left the beach a long time ago, but it was the most beautiful sunset, and she was busy painting it. Her friend Serena was getting restless, 'It must [2]_____ finished by now, surely Paula?' she asked. But Paula was lost in her creative world, inspired by the deep red sky. 'A beautiful scene like this just [3]_____ be missed, Serena,' she told her friend. 'For all we know, this painting [4]_____ have been sold in my art gallery by the end of the month. And then we can go on holiday!' Serena eyed her friend's creative work, and had to admit it was extremely good; it could have [5]_____ painted by someone much more experienced than her friend. She was convinced that Paula [6]_____ be accepted at art college next year. With luck, she too might have [7]_____ all her graphic design exams by the end of the year, and would be able to start her own creative career.

6 Listen and speak

🔊 Work with a partner and listen to the second part of the interview.

Student A: Draw the radio presenter's first metaphor.

Student B: Draw the radio presenter's second metaphor.

Students A & B: Compare your drawings. Discuss how Jane Davis invites the radio host to think differently about a situation that is difficult for him.

Think of a situation that is difficult for you, for example, one that makes you feel nervous or angry.

1 Draw a metaphor of how you feel in this situation.
2 Draw a metaphor for how you would like to feel in this situation.
3 How do your feelings about the difficult situation change when you move qualities from the second picture into the first? Discuss with a partner.

Culture in mind

7 Read

(a) Look at the pictures of three buildings from around the world. Which one do you think is (or was originally):

1. a hotel?
2. a meeting place for a city council?
3. a private home?

(b) Read the texts quickly to check your ideas.

Inspired buildings

The twentieth century, perhaps more than any other, marked a period where architects experimented with form and took their inspiration from various sources. That they can do this is partly because of modern materials and building techniques which allow buildings to be built that could never have taken shape in earlier times. Here is a selection of our favourites.

a) Casa Batlló, located in the heart of Barcelona in Spain, was designed by Antoni Gaudí and built in the years 1905–1907. The local name for the six-storey building is *Casa dels ossos* (the house of bones), and it was originally designed for a middle-class family and situated in a prosperous district of Barcelona. It is now a museum.

The building is remarkable, like virtually everything Gaudí designed. It seems that his goal was to avoid straight lines completely – the front of the house is all wavy lines. The ground floor in particular is astonishing, with irregular oval windows and flowing sculpted stone work. There are various thoughts about the symbolism: some people say it is a poetic vision of the sea, whilst others say carnival scenes are represented. Most likely, however, is that Gaudí was thinking of a huge dragon, with the roof being the dragon's curved back, given that this was a recurring theme in his work.

b) The **Burj al-Arab hotel in Dubai** was started in 1994, and its doors were opened to guests on December 1, 1999. It is 321 metres high and was built to resemble the sail of a *dhow*, a type of Arabian sailing boat. The hotel stands on an artificial island 280 metres out from Jumeirah beach, and is connected to the mainland by a private curving bridge. Near the top is a helipad, and extending from the other side of the hotel, 200 metres above the ocean, is a restaurant. The Burj al-Arab features the tallest atrium lobby in the world (180 metres high).

Architect Tom Wright stated that the hotel was intended to be 'a building that would become synonymous with the name of the country'.

The Burj al-Arab does not have ordinary rooms – it has 202 suites, the smallest of which occupies an area of 169 square metres, and the largest 780 square metres. It is one of the most expensive hotels in the world, with prices ranging from $1,000 to $28,000 a night.

c) City Hall in London is the headquarters of the Greater London Authority and the Mayor of London. It stands on the south bank of the River Thames. Designed by Norman Foster, it opened in July 2002.

The building has an unusual bulbous shape, which reduces the surface area and thus improves energy efficiency since less heat is lost to the outside. It has been variously compared to Darth Vader's helmet, a misshapen egg or a motorcycle helmet. The building has no front or back in conventional terms, but derives its shape from a modified sphere.

A 500 metre walkway goes right to the very top of the ten-storey building, where there is an exhibition and meeting space called 'London's Living Room', with an open viewing deck which is occasionally open to the public. The walkway provides views of the interior of the building, and is intended to symbolise transparency of government. A similar device was used by Foster in his design for the rebuilt Reichstag in Germany.

c Read the texts again and answer the questions.

1 Which building resembles:
   – a fictional animal?
   – a means of transport?
   – something you wear on your head?

2 Which building:
   – was the most recently opened of the three?
   – set a world record?
   – is called something else by local people?

d Do you know any other building (local or worldwide) that you think is different / inventive / creative? Tell the class what you know about it/them.

8 Write

a Read the extract from a book on learning. What metaphors do the authors mention?

Any learning experience provides a valuable opportunity to revisit fundamental principles of growth and change. Over the past 25 years, we have complemented our academic research into the brain and learning with practical tests. We've challenged ourselves continuously to learn new things – particularly things for which we'd been told, as children, we had little or no talent. We've learned many new skills such as singing, swimming, ballroom dancing, tennis, languages, martial arts, drawing and juggling.

Anyone of these subjects could provide a fertile metaphor for exploring the art of learning and life. But juggling offers something special. We chose juggling as the focus of our book because learning anything involves keeping a number of things 'up in the air' at the same time, because 'dropping the balls' provides an ideal metaphor for gracefully coping with mistakes, which we consider one of life's most important abilities. Juggling also provides a sense of inner quiet in the midst of activity, a special experience of mind and body in harmony. And juggling's essential light-heartedness encourages easy access to the fundamental human learning modality of play.

b The authors say that a number of skills they learned could be used as metaphors for learning. Work with a partner to create similes or metaphors using the skills 1–5 from the text in Exercise 8a.

1 Swimming *Learning is like swimming – as soon as you stop it there is the danger that you drown.*
2 Ballroom dancing ....
3 Tennis ....
4 Languages ....
5 Martial arts ....

c Work in a small group. Make a list of words or phrases which might give interesting stimuli for creating metaphors, for example: *freedom, love, friendship, going to university, studying for a test, reading*.

d Decide on one of the words or phrases from Exercise 8c. Each member of the group now writes down as many metaphors or similes for that word or phrase. Write each one on a separate piece of paper.

Freedom is choosing your own paths
Freedom is walking on a tightrope without a net

e Discuss which you think are the strongest metaphors and similes. Arrange them to form a poem.

For your portfolio

8 Virtual worlds

* Cleft sentences review
* Vocabulary: money
* Vocabulary: word building

1 Read and listen

(a) What do you know about virtual worlds on the Internet?

(b) What do you think you would find in a virtual world?

(c) Do you think that people would pay to enter a virtual world? Read the texts quickly to check your ideas.

Explaining the modern world
The Entropia Universe

Now, $10,000 might seem quite a sum for an egg, especially when it's not even real. But that's the price that Jon Neverdie Jacobs has recently paid for the Unique Green Atrox Queen Egg, a virtual egg dreamed up by the creators of The Entropia Universe. It was Jacobs who made the headlines when he paid around $100,000 for an asteroid space resort in the virtual universe, with plans to turn it into the world's first virtual nightclub Neverdie. Jacobs also sees his recent purchase as a future investment and claims that whatever hatches out of the egg, people will be happy to pay good money to enter his club and see it. Whether he took out a loan in the real world to be able to make this investment is not known.

So, what do you need to know about The Entropia Universe?

☐ The Entropia Universe is a virtual world unlike any other; a world of science fiction set in a distant future and based on a planet called Calypso. Players from the real world visit this Internet playground to live out their alternative lives as they help colonise the dangerous wilderness that surrounds them.

☐ Entropia was the brainchild of a group of Swedish computer boffins who decided to see if they could manage to create a three dimensional virtual world that could be placed on the Internet. They did manage, but they had no money to make it happen. But four years later their project got the green light when they received the financial backing they needed.

☐ Although there are various activities to keep you busy on Calypso, what most inhabitants do first is to find themselves a profession. Then they can think about buying their virtual house or paying a visit to a virtual beauty salon or a virtual nightclub or doing any of the other activities that make life bearable out there.

☐ Hunting the ferocious wild animals and mining the precious minerals found on the planet are two of the most popular professions on Calypso. Other ways of earning a living include making tools, manufacturing clothing and hairdressing.

☐ Entropia has its very own economy and its own currency, the PED (Project Entropia Dollars) which all deals are negotiated in. Players transfer real world money into PED which they then use to pay for their life on Calypso, using a PED cash card. However, the virtual items inside Entropia do have a real value in the outside world, and careful business deals mean that players can actually make real money there. PED can be converted into dollars any time at a rate of 10PED to 1US$.

☐ You can actually take part in The Entropia Universe with no money at all, although it is by spending cash that you really expand your options. Most people who do not open their own account in Entropia treat the service as little more than a fancy 3-D virtual chat room. You are free to explore the universe but you'll have to wear the bright orange jumpsuit, given to all new players, wherever you go.

☐ As soon as you become an inhabitant of planet Calypso you'll need to choose your avatar – that is, your online image. There are a number of things about your avatar that you can change, from skin and eye colour to body fitness and body piercing as well as an infinite number of hairstyles. The more money you are willing to spend, the fancier you can look.

☐ What's so impressive about The Entropia Universe is the number of participants; currently more than 600,000 representing over 220 countries from planet Earth. Many real-life friendships have been formed as well as several marriages.

☐ A number of players insist that it's a good way to make money. However, the reality of Entropia's economic system is that most people end up paying more than they earn and it's not uncommon to find participants who are paying up to $200 a month into their PED account. This might not be the most economical way of spending one's free time. However, some people claim that for them the fact that they can escape the realities of their earthbound life and become a different person with a completely different life for a few hours every week is worth the investment, even if they don't get any interest rates on it.

d) Read the text and write the numbers of the questions in the correct place. There is one question you do not need to use.

1 What do people do in a virtual world?
2 How do I represent myself there?
3 So what's the future for the Universe?
4 How did it all start?
5 How do you pay for it all?

6 What can I do if I've got no or little money?
7 Will I get lonely there?
8 What is it?
9 Why is it proving so popular?
10 What kind of jobs do people do on Calypso?

e) Read the text again and listen. Mark the statements *T* (true), *F* (false) or *N* (not in the text). Correct the false statements.

1 Entropia is a virtual playground developed by rich Swedish computer scientists. ☐
2 The majority of players do not immediately go for entertainment when they first enter Entropia. ☐
3 Manufacturing clothes is among the professions most frequently chosen by Entropia's inhabitants. ☐
4 It is obligatory for players who want their own identity and looks in Entropia to open their own account. ☐
5 A number of players claim that they are earning a living from the game. ☐

2 Vocabulary

Money

a) Match the words 1–10 from the text with their definitions.

1 purchase
2 take out a loan
3 earn a living
4 economy
5 currency
6 cash card
7 open an account
8 economic
9 economical
10 interest rate

a a country's system of trade and industry by which its wealth is created and used
b a special plastic card that you can use to take money out of a bank
c to make an arrangement with a bank to keep your money there
d borrow a sum of money, often from a bank, that has to be paid back
e relating to trade, industry and money
f do a job to make money to buy things you need in life
g not using a lot of money, fuel, energy etc.
h a percentage that a bank or a person gets from someone who borrows money
i the money that is used in a particular country at a particular time
j something that you buy (also: to buy)

b) Complete each sentence using a word from Exercise 2a.

1 The country has recovered from the _economic_ crisis.
2 They all congratulated their mother on the .... of the new house.
3 I had to buy a new computer – it wouldn't have been .... to have the old one repaired.
4 Nowadays many students have to .... to be able to afford to go to university.
5 The .... on the loan we had to take out has gone up by 4 per cent since last year.
6 An increase in tourism will have a very positive effect on the ....

Discussion box

Work in pairs or small groups. Discuss these questions together.

1 What do you think of Entropia? What positive and negative aspects do you think there are about it?
2 Some people claim that virtual worlds like Entropia 'should be forbidden' because they are harmful. Do you agree? Why / Why not?
3 What do you think of people who invest their real money on virtual purchases?
4 Have you ever played a virtual reality game? How was it different or similar to The Entropia Universe?

3 Grammar

Cleft sentences with *what* and *it* review

(a) Look at these sentences. Say them without the *what* construction.

What's so impressive about the Entropia Universe is the number of participants.

What most inhabitants do first is find themselves a profession.

(b) Underline the information in the two sentences in Exercise 3a, that is the main focus of the sentence.

(c) Complete the rule with *beginning* or *end*.

> **Rule:**
> - Cleft sentences with *what* shift the focus of attention to the information at the _____ of the sentence.

(d) Rewrite these sentences as cleft sentences with *what*.

1 People spend real money on purchasing virtual property.

    What most people do is spend real money on purchasing virtual property.

2 I would never transfer money into a virtual account.

3 Some players don't care how much money they spend on virtual reality games.

4 Some new cars are very economical and that's good.

5 People spend money on these games – I don't understand why.

6 I don't want to make things difficult.

(e) Look at these sentences. Say them without the *it* construction.

It was Jacobs who made the headlines in October 2005.

It is by spending cash that you really expand your options.

(f) Underline the information in the two sentences in Exercise 3e that is the main focus of the sentence.

(g) Complete the rule with *beginning* or *end*.

> **Rule:**
> - Cleft sentences with *it* shift the focus of attention to the information at the _____ of the sentence. (These sentences are often used to correct information that is wrong.)

Look

The subject of the sentence is *it* so the verb is always *was*. You can say:

- *It was the Americans who made the first personal computer, the Altair, in 1975.*
- *Not ~~They were the Americans~~ ...*

(h) Correct the information in the sentences. Use an *it* cleft and the correct information in brackets.

1 Brazil won the World Cup in 2006. (Italy)
   No – it was Italy that won the World Cup in 2006.

2 Jon Jacobs invented Entropia. (Swedish scientists)

3 Everyone playing Entropia has to wear an orange jumpsuit. (new players)

4 Neil Armstrong was the first man in space. (Yuri Gagarin)

5 The Wright Brothers were the first people to fly. (Santos Dumont)

6 Superman turns green when he's angry. (The Hulk)

4 Listen

(a) Think of the best holiday you have ever had. As you remember that holiday, notice what you remember most strongly: Images? Smells? Sounds?

(b) Work in a small group. Ask and answer questions about your holiday memories. Are images, smells and sounds equally important for each of you?

c 🔊 Listen and (circle) the correct answers.

1 Remote Media makes it possible to enjoy images and smells of far away holiday locations:
   a without leaving home
   b at your nearest travel agent
   c after you have been there only once

2 The first such multi-sensory holiday experience was in Egypt and includes:
   a famous sights and camel rides
   b deep sea diving in the Red Sea
   c sunsets in the Valley of the Kings

3 The aroma system was developed by a company who even managed to provide the smell of:
   a sea water
   b human breath
   c Egyptian lotus flowers

4 The system has already been introduced in one of Thompson's branches. Customers' reactions have been:
   a quite critical
   b overwhelmingly positive
   c rather positive

5 For the time being the system will mainly be used to promote:
   a virtual holidays
   b the smell of exotic spices and herbs
   c real holidays

d 🔊 Listen to the interview again. Put the interview points in the correct order. Write 1–6 in the boxes.

a The services of the suppliers of the aroma system were previously used by Madame Tussaud's. ☐

b A top manager stressed that the system helps customers with making the right choice for their holiday. ☐

c Special filming equipment is used that allows viewers a 'full surround' holiday feeling. ☐

d The virtual holiday experience is almost as good as really going to those places. ☐

e It is intended to extend the system to promote other holiday places in the future. ☐

f The system requires people to wear a special headset and lasts less than five minutes. ☐

5 Speak

Work in pairs or small groups. Discuss these questions together.

a Imagine Remote Media wanted to create an up-to-date virtual holiday package for your country. Which places would you include in a three and a half minute promotional video? Which smells and sounds would you include?

b Imagine it was possible to implant 'virtual holiday memories' into the human brain, and people didn't need to go on holiday any more. What might be the advantages for the future of our planet? What dangers might that cause? Would you enjoy such a holiday?

6 Vocabulary
Word building

a Look at the sentences from the listening in Exercise 4 and (circle) the correct word. Use a dictionary if you need to.

1 ... without leaving the *comfortable* / *comfort* / *comforting* of their nearest travel agent.

2 It combines three *dimensions* / *dimension* / *dimensional* imagery with aroma *technology* / *technological*.

3 A *special* / *specially* / *speciality* camera was used to film the different locations.

4 ...the smell of Kylie Minogue's *breath* / *breathe* / *breathing* ...

5 ... where it's met with *consider* / *considerable* / *considering* approval.

6 ... they can *create* / *creative* / *creation* and *promote* / *promotion* / *promotional* a growing number of other locations.

7 ... a virtual holiday implanted into our *memories* / *memoirs* / *memorials*.

b Look at the words in italics in Exercise 6a. Which part of speech is each one? Choose from a verb, adjective, adverb or noun.

c Read about the film *Total Recall*. Use the words in the box to form a word that fits into each space.

| trust | real | construct | imagine | horrible |
| die | record | fly | free | constant |

Total Recall

When your memory is no longer
¹ *trustworthy* how can you know what
² .... is any more? On earth
Arnold Schwarzenegger is a ³ ....
worker who can't stop dreaming about
Mars. A trip to a sinister memory
transplant service for an ⁴ ....
holiday on Mars goes ⁵ ....
wrong and when he returns he finds
things are not quite the same. It seems
everyone wants him ⁶ ....
including his wife, friends and several
strangers too. A ⁷ .... left by his
'other self' tells him to get a
⁸ .... to Mars and join up with
the underground ⁹ .... fighters.
The reality of the situation is
¹⁰ .... in question. Who is he?
What is real and what is not?

7 Listen

a 🔊 Listen to the song without looking at the words. Does the singer have a positive or negative view of virtual worlds?

Virtual World
by Andru Donalds

Nowadays so many things have changed
I can feel the cold.
Don't be blind and hope to realise:
You're just a morphing soul
In a virtual world. (homeless heart, left alone, looking for a home)
Children hypnotised in front of a TV
Playing lonely, just with best friend TFT*
People talking, chatting all around the world,
Ignoring time and the ones they will need
When they sit in the cold

[Chorus]
Think about if that's the way life should be (you need a touch)
You'll never get that thrill from talking to a TV (it means so much)
I just doubt, that is the way you want to get old
Without the feeling of love, you are lost
In a virtual world (homeless heart, left alone, looking for a hold)

But from the very start, it was a world away,
Looking for the digital horizons.
I can trust in love and my soul
Instead of a virtual world
Night and day, I see these people on the street (they need a touch)
Cyber junkies, losing sense of time, (it means so much)
Surrounded by people without a bit of soul,
Ignoring time and the ones who will help
When they sit in the cold

[Chorus]
Think about if that's the way life should be, (you need a touch)
You'll never get that thrill from talking to a TV (it means so much)
I just doubt, that is the way you want to get old.
Without the feeling of love, you'll be lost
In a virtual world

* TFT = a special kind of TV screen

Did you know ...?

Andru Donalds is a Jamaican whose father was a professor of theology and psychology and who wanted him to take up an academic career. But Andru preferred music. After several years struggling, he released his first album in 1995. It was produced by Eric Foster White, who has also produced music for Whitney Houston, Hi-Five and Britney Spears.

So far, he has released five albums.

b 🔊 Listen again and correct six words in the song which are wrong.

c In which part of the song does the singer suggest:

1   that people can become addicted to virtual worlds?
2   that machines are inhuman?
3   that children are controlled by television?
4   that human emotions are more valuable than virtual worlds?

8 Write

(a) Read the letter quickly. What is its purpose? What is the relationship between the writer and the addressee?

(b) Cathy uses several informal and colloquial expressions. Find informal expressions in the text with these meanings.

1 joking _____ *kidding* _____
2 children _____
3 home, flat _____
4 very easy _____
5 get something to eat

_____
6 go quickly, rush _____
7 assume _____
8 strange _____
9 find me _____

Day 10 in my new flat

Hi Chris,

Phew! Finally I've managed to sit down and do what I've wanted to for quite some time – write to my favourite brother (relax – you'd still be my favourite even if I had six!!!) Well, I guess you can imagine how busy I am with enrolling for the right courses at university, getting the books our tutors want us to read (they're demanding, I tell you) and keeping up with my extremely tiring social life (kidding, of course, but I've got two friends already who are on the same courses and are really nice!).

Anyway, the reason for my writing is of course that I want to thank you for the wonderful present. I must say that I did find it a bit funny that you gave me a cash card for an online game as a present, but after all this isn't the first time you've surprised me (remember when we were kids and you insisted we went swimming in the river near the house on 1 December? Freezing cold!). Seriously, thank you very, very much. I did enter Virtropia the very first evening I was in my new place, and had great fun choosing an identity and a profession for myself. So, watch out for a gold digger the next time you play. Or am I that hunter who always hunts before dusk, or maybe the woodcutter who lives high up in a tree house in the valley with the white buffaloes? (Won't tell you who I am, of course, you have to find out for yourself!) Hooray! Piece of cake to get myself the outfit I wanted – thanks to your generosity, and the £50 in my account, of course!

Must go now – course starting in 40 mins. Still need to grab a bite before I dash off!

Bye for now,

Cathy

P.S: Call me at 9 tonight. Let's enter Virtropia together, shall we? Curious to see how long it takes you to check me out ...

P.P.S: One of my two new friends is Jessica. She's really nice and she keeps asking me questions about you. (She wouldn't if she met you ...)

(c) Work with a partner and discuss the questions.

1 What is unusual about the date and the address in this letter?

2 The letter begins with 'Hi, Chris' and ends with 'Bye for now, Cathy'. What other beginnings or endings can we use in informal letters?

3 What kind of language can you find in the letter that is typical of informal writing? Give examples.

4 What do you notice about the use of contracted forms?

5 What do you notice about the use of brackets (...)?

(d) You have received the following invitation from a very good friend of yours who lives in the UK. You would love to accept the invitation, but unfortunately you have to refuse it. Write a letter or email to let your friend know and give your reasons. Add some of your recent news.

FOR SPECIAL FRIENDS ONLY:

CELEBRATE WITH ME
I'm 18!!! FINALLY!!!
Let's party!!!
Where: in our garden
When: Saturday 14 June 7pm

Love, Hilary

For your portfolio

Module 2 Check your progress

1 Grammar

a Put the verbs in brackets into the correct form.

1 The teacher told us _to study_ for the exam the next day. (study)
2 They confessed .... the car. (steal)
3 He apologised for .... to the party late. (get)
4 He claimed .... some important people in the government. (know)
5 He advised us .... to the police immediately. (go)
6 They offered .... the money back. (pay)
7 She denied .... in the test. (cheat)
8 I admitted .... to pass myself off as someone else. (try)

☐ **7**

b (Circle) the correct option.

1 You're going to travel round the world on your own? You *can be* / (*must be*) mad!
2 I can't find my wallet. I *must lose* / *must have lost* it somewhere.
3 He failed the exam. He *can't have studied* / *might have studied* enough.
4 She's on television almost every day – you *must know* / *must have known* who she is.
5 I'm sorry, I'm a stranger here, so I *can't help* / *can't have helped* you.
6 But we've met five times before – you *will have* / *can't have* forgotten my name!
7 It's strange she isn't here yet. She *might miss* / *might have missed* the bus.
8 Don't phone me at 8 tomorrow morning – *I'll leave* / *I'll have left* for school by then.

☐ **7**

c Rewrite each sentence, beginning with the word given.

1 A hairdresser cut my hair.
I _had my hair cut._
2 My father's car is being repaired at the garage.
My father ....
3 Someone has designed these invitations for me.
I ....
4 The doctors took her appendix out.
She ....
5 Someone is going to decorate their living room.
They ....
6 His photograph was taken.
He ....

☐ **5**

d Complete with the correct form of the verb in brackets.

1 His new CD will _be released_ next month. (release)
2 A new library might .... in a few years' time. (build)
3 The completed form must .... before the end of this month. (send)
4 The window might .... in last night's storm. (break)
5 I didn't know about this – I think I should .... about it. (tell)
6 I'm really sorry to tell you this, but your computer can't .... (fix)
7 This note is very hard to read – it must .... in a hurry. (write)

☐ **6**

e Rewrite each sentence, starting with the words given.

1 The most difficult thing is getting an idea.
It's _getting an idea that's the most difficult thing._
2 I don't understand why people want to play computer games.
What ....
3 People wasting their time and money makes me really angry.
It's ....
4 Being careful with your money – that's the important thing.
What ....
5 The really interesting bit was the end of the film.
It ....
6 I don't like sitting in front of a computer for a long time.
It ....
7 The difficult thing for me was trying to understand the rules of the game.
What ....
8 Virtual worlds will be more and more common in the future.
What ....

☐ **7**

2 Vocabulary

a Complete the puzzle by writing a word to replace each phrase in italics.

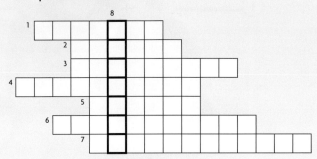

1 The army *entered the other country* to try to take it over.
2 The two presidents signed *a written agreement between the two countries.*
3 The army needed more soldiers, so they *got* more men *to join.*
4 The war produced a lot of *people who were killed or injured.*
5 There was an important *fight between two armies* here 100 years ago.
6 In the end, one army *stopped fighting and admitted defeat.*
7 Finally, the two countries started peace *discussions to reach an agreement.*
8 I don't want my country ever to *officially announce* war on another country.

[ ] 8

b Complete by writing one word in each space.

1 No money, no friends, nothing to do – it's the ___story___ of my life.
2 He tried to tell us how his parents were poor and he was bullied at school – a real _____ story.
3 You only got 10 per cent in the test because your pen broke? That's a _____ story!
4 Well, to _____ a long story short, we didn't get home until 3am in the morning.
5 OK, now let's listen to Jane and we can hear her _____ of the story.
6 I don't believe a word of it! You're just _____ up a story, aren't you?
7 No, you can't go out tonight! _____ of story!
8 So you're saying it was his fault, not yours? It's always the _____ old story, isn't it?

[ ] 7

c Complete by writing one or more words in each space.

1 I was so surprised! I didn't know what had ___hit___ me.
2 I'm really nervous! I have _____ in my stomach.
3 I'm so angry! This kind of thing really makes my blood _____ .
4 I think he's a bit mad, you know? I reckon he's got a screw _____ or something.
5 Calm down! Don't get so angry! Just keep your _____ on, OK?
6 She was so happy, you know, on top _____ .
7 He was really embarrassed! He didn't know _____ himself.
8 This is a waste of my time! I feel like I'm banging my head against _____ .

[ ] 7

d Complete with the correct form of the word in brackets.

1 This book is quite old, but it isn't very ___valuable___ . (value)
2 Designing advertisements requires quite a lot of _____ . (create)
3 She's a great cook – her _____ is chicken tikka masala. (special)
4 Why do you have to be so _____ all the time? (argument)
5 A _____ number of people bought the book. (consider)
6 I can still recall the first time I heard this song – it was a _____ experience. (memory)
7 The only way to find the problem is to check everything _____ . (system)

[ ] 6

How did you do?

Tick (✓) a box for each section.

Total score:	☺	☹	☹
[ ] 60	Very good	OK	Not very good
Grammar	25 – 32	15 – 24	less than 15
Vocabulary	20 – 28	14 – 19	less than 14

Module 3
Alone and together

YOU WILL LEARN ABOUT ...

- World-famous superheroes ....
- Habits and gestures ....
- Winning and losing in sport ....
- Landmarks in Brasília ....
- What it's like to live alone in the wild ....
- Why we copy behaviour ....

✳ Can you match each picture with a topic?

YOU WILL LEARN HOW TO ...

Speak

- Talk about the advantages and limitations of learning through imitation
- Discuss the importance of empathy in cross-cultural communication
- Talk about sports events and athletes.
- Give a talk
- Talk about superheroes
- Design and present a team of superheroes
- Discuss what it would be like to live completely on your own
- Talk about what to take to survive on a desert island

Write

- A discursive composition
- A description of a sporting event for a school magazine
- A film review
- A leaflet for a summer project

Read

- An article explaining the biological reasons for how we understand other people
- Stories about dramatic sporting failures
- An article on superheroes.
- The diary of a scientist living on his own in the wilderness

Listen

- An expert talking about our communication skills
- A discussion about cheating in sport
- A teenager's presentation about architecture in Brasília
- An audition for a TV reality show
- Interviews with teenagers about being on their own

Use grammar

Can you match the names of the grammar points with the examples?

Hedging

Boosting

could, be able to, manage to

Negative inversion

Mixed conditionals

Alternatives to *if*

He was hurt but he **was able to** play on.

If I **had never come** here, I **wouldn't know** how valuable solitude is.

This discovery has **unquestionably** been one of the most important steps forward in recent neuroscience.

This **seems to be** an area that is worth investigating.

I'd just have to phone someone, **otherwise** I'd go crazy!

Under no circumstances can I recommend this film.

Use vocabulary

Can you think of two more examples for each topic?

Habits and gestures	Success and failure	From human to hero	Expressions with *time*
blink	succeed	superhuman strength	make time
yawn	fail	short-sighted	time's up
....	....	....	....
....	....	....	....

61

9 Understanding others

★ Hedging and boosting
★ Vocabulary: habits and gestures

1 Read and listen

(a) Work with a partner. Look at the photo and the title of the text. Discuss what you think the article is about.

(b) Read the text quickly and check your answers.

(c) 🔊 Read the text again and listen. Match the statements 1–6 with the paragraphs A–E. Write in the boxes. Two statements are in the same paragraph.

1 Mirror neurons cause humans to copy other people's behaviour, and to feel empathy with them. ☐

2 Lack in social behaviour might be caused by problems in someone's mirror-neuron-system. ☐

3 The scientific importance of the discovery of mirror neurons. ☐

4 The key role mirror neurons play especially in language learning. ☐

5 The discovery that the same neurons get activated in a monkey's brain whether the monkey does an action himself or watches someone else do the action. ☐

6 The claim that mirror neurons might be the reason why some people seem to enjoy being violent. ☐

(d) 🔊 Read the text and listen again. Answer the questions.

1 What was the surprising observation the scientists made when studying monkeys?

2 What have scientists found out about the role of mirror neurons in learning?

3 In what way do mirror neurons explain the way people live together?

4 What have scientists learned about the processes in the brain that are activated by language?

A revealing reflection

Mirror neurons are providing stunning insights into everything from how we learnt to walk to how we empathise with others

You know how it is when you see someone yawn and you start yawning too? Or how hard it is to be amongst people laughing and not laugh yourself (even if you don't find something funny)? Perhaps you've wondered why that is. Well, apparently it's because we have mirror neurons in our brains.

[A] Some years ago, three scientists at a university in Italy were studying monkeys – more specifically, they were looking at what happens in a monkey's brain when it performs certain actions. They attached electrodes to a monkey's head, and watched what happened when it did things like pick up a raisin and eat it. But what the scientists discovered was quite different from what they had expected. One day, during a break, one of the scientists himself picked up a raisin and ate it, and as the monkey watched him do so, the neurons in its brain fired in exactly the same way as they had done when the monkey itself ate a raisin. Stunned by what they had observed, the three men replicated the experiment many times, always with the same result, and they realised that they had stumbled across something quite new. They published a series of papers in which they called the neurons they had studied 'mirror neurons', and this has unquestionably been one of the most important steps forward in recent neuroscience.

[B] Put simply, the existence of mirror neurons suggests that every time we see someone else do something – smile, smell a flower, or yawn – our brains imitate it, whether or not we actually perform the same action. This explains a great deal about how we learn to smile, talk, walk, dance or play sports. But the idea goes further: mirror neurons not only appear to explain physical actions, they also tell us that there is a biological basis for the way we understand other people and empathise with them – and why, perhaps, we sometimes don't.

[C] Mirror neurons can undoubtedly be found all over our brains, but especially in the areas which relate to our ability to use language, to understand how other people feel, and to understand other people's intentions. We appear to use mirror neurons to learn just about everything we do: when we're babies, they help us learn how to smile, how to walk and so on, and when we're older, how to give facial expression to subtle emotions or how to learn complex dance movements. Most remarkably, perhaps, researchers have found that mirror neurons relate strongly to language – a group of researchers discovered that if they gave people sentences to listen to (for example: 'The hand took hold of the ball'), the same mirror neurons were triggered as when the action was actually performed (in this example, actually taking hold of a ball).

[D] As we might expect – since mirror neurons are so basic to our understanding, learning and development – any problems with mirror neurons may well result in problems with behaviour. Considerable research has been carried out which suggests that

people with social and behavioural problems have mirror neurons which are not fully functioning. The result is an ability to understand what others mean through their expressions and gestures, but not to empathise with the emotions behind them. However, it is not yet known exactly how these discoveries might lead to treatments for social disorders.

[E] It is thought that mirror neurons can also explain a great deal about the development in humans of what we term 'culture'. For about 200,000 years, the human brain seems not to have changed in size – but it is now believed that about 50,000 years ago, the human brain began to change genetically to incorporate our present mirroring ability, and this was what allowed us to move forward so quickly in communication and learning. But naturally, mirror neurons sometimes produce unwanted results and behaviours. Some research suggests that key neurons are involved in an association of pleasure and success with hurting other people – for example, in many video games. If this is correct, then what is termed 'imitative' violence may be almost beyond the control of some people, leading to a driving force that no society would want to encourage.

Nevertheless, research into mirror neurons seems to provide us with ever more information concerning how humans behave and interact. Indeed, it may turn out to be the equivalent for neuroscience of what Einstein's theory of relativity was for physics. And the next time you feel the urge to cough in the cinema when someone else does – well, perhaps you'll understand why.

e Find words or phrases in the text with these meanings.

1 nerve cells that carry information between the brain and other parts of the body (paragraph 1)

2 make or do something again in exactly the same way (paragraph 2)

3 the scientific study of the nervous system (paragraph 2)

4 to be able to understand well how someone else feels (paragraph 3)

5 small but important (paragraph 4)

6 problems in someone's behaviour towards others (paragraph 5)

7 to include something as part of something larger (paragraph 6)

8 the energy that makes something move (paragraph 6)

Discussion box

Work in small groups. Discuss these questions together.

1 Give examples of areas where you think imitation can be a powerful learning tool.
Are there other areas where learning through imitating others might not be so efficient?

2 Why do mirror neurons play a significant role in understanding others?

3 Why are emphatic skills so important when people coming from different cultures meet or live together?

2 Listen

🔊 Listen to an expert talking about human communication skills. Complete the sentences.

1 Building rapport with another person is about giving them the feeling that you are on the same .... as them.

2 Mirroring is a technique in which you imitate a person's micro-behaviour, such as .... and gestures.

3 When using the technique one should not .... with mirroring, but do it gently and respectfully.

4 Mirroring can help to build very good rapport with another person, so it is your .... not to misuse the other person's trust.

5 The technique can be used to imitate people's physical behaviour, but we can also mirror .... if we watch the way they speak and use words.

6 If doctors use the techniques in their communication, they can better understand a patient's real ....

3 | Vocabulary

Habits and gestures

a) Match the words and the pictures.

blink   cough   tilt your head   bite your nails   fiddle with your hair   rub your forehead
stroke your chin   rub your hands together   yawn   fold your hands behind your head

 ①  ②  ③ 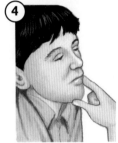 ④  ⑤

rub your forehead _____ _____ _____ _____

 ⑥  ⑦  ⑧ 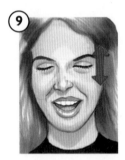 ⑨  ⑩

_____ _____ _____ _____ _____

b) Which action(s) in Exercise 3a do people sometimes do in the following situations:

1 when they're nervous?
2 when they don't like what's happening?
3 when they're thinking hard?
4 when they're tired?
5 when they're upset?

c) Work with a partner. Answer the questions about the actions in Exercise 3a.

1 Which actions can we sometimes control / sometimes not control?
2 Do you think any of the actions are done more by men than women (and vice versa)?
3 Which things (if any) are not polite in your country/culture?

4 | Speak

Work in a group of three. Student A chooses a topic from the box and talks about it with Student B for three minutes. Student C listens and ticks (✓) which gestures in the table that Student A and B use. After three minutes, change roles. Do this until each student in your group has listened. Now compare the notes in your table and talk about what you have noticed.

sport   music   holidays   family   films

	Student A	Student B	Student C
Moves head to right			
Moves head to left			
Moves left hand to left			
Moves right hand to right			
Fiddles with hair			
Blinks			
Touches face			
Nods head			

5 Grammar

Hedging and boosting

(a) Look at the sentences from the text in Exercise 1. In two of these sentences, the speaker makes a claim very assertively. In the other two, the speaker makes a claim more cautiously. Which are which?

1 *Mirror neurons can **undoubtedly** be found all over our brains.*

2 *We **appear to use** them to learn just about everything we do.*

3 *For about 200,000 years, the human brain **seems not to have changed** in size.*

4 *This has **unquestionably** been one of the most important steps forward in recent neuroscience.*

(b) Complete the rules with *direct*, *formal* and *avoid*.

Rules:

- We often want to ¹........ making statements that are too strong, for example, when we present ideas about something that we are still working on. In these situations, we can use a technique called **hedging**. Instead of *this is* we can say '*this **seems to be** ...*', '*this **appears to be** ...*', '*this **is believed to be** ...*', and '*this **is thought to be** ...*'

- When we do want to make a more ²........ statement, we can use a technique called **boosting**. Instead of *this is ...* we can say '*this is **undoubtedly / unquestionably / definitely** ...*'.

- These structures are especially common in ³........ written texts.

(c) Rewrite the sentences using the word in brackets.

1 It is the most important discovery of the century. (definitely)

   It is definitely the most important discovery of the century.

2 This is an area that is worth investigating. (seem)

3 Further research in this area would be a waste of time. (unquestionably)

4 Some great advances have been made. (appear)

5 Understanding more about how the brain works can be useful. (undoubtedly)

6 Scientists have made enormous progress in this area. (believed)

Look

Remember that adverbs usually come:
- **after** the verb *to be* (*This is undoubtedly ...*)
- **before** other verbs (*It definitely needs to ... .*)
- **between** auxiliaries and participles (*This has unquestionably been ...*)
- **between** infinitives, participles and auxiliaries (*This has undoubtedly been ... / This will undoubtedly be ...*)

---

6 Speak

Work with a partner.

Student A: Use hedging phrases to report (seriously or jokingly) about one of the headlines in the list.

Student B: Listen, and then use boosting phrases to comment on the importance of the new research. Then change roles.

Neurons discovered that explain snoring

New fuel found that can replace petrol

Women now own 46 per cent of businesses in the US

Men have genes that make them good at finding their way, say scientists

RESEARCH SAYS THAT TELEVISION DESTROYS BRAIN CELLS

Scientists prove that laughter extends life expectancy

A: *It appears scientists have found new neurons in the human brain that seem to explain why some people snore.*

B: *Really?*

A: *Yes. The human brain seems to have developed the neurons at the beginning of the last century, because people had to listen to too many long, boring conversations. It is believed that the discovery of these neurons will lead to completely new ways of treating people who snore.*

B: *Amazing! This research is undoubtedly a major step forward in medicine! It's as important as discoveries like penicillin.*

Literature in mind

7 Read

THE NUMBER ONE BESTSELLER

YANN MARTEL

Life of Pi

winner of
THE Man BOOKER PRIZE 2002

Life of Pi

After the tragic sinking of a cargo ship which was carrying an entire zoo, one lifeboat remains on the wild, blue Pacific. The only survivors from the wreck are a sixteen-year-old boy named Pi, a hyena, a zebra (with a broken leg), a female orang-utan ... and a 450-pound Royal Bengal tiger. The tiger eats the other animals — and then there's only it and the boy.

In this extract, the boy Pi has seen a petrol tanker coming towards the lifeboat that he is on, and believes at first that he and the tiger are going to be saved.

(a) Read the extract quickly to find the answer to these questions.

1　Who is Richard Parker?

2　Does the tanker hit the lifeboat or not?

I realised with horror that the tanker was not simply coming our way — it was in fact bearing down on us. The bow was a vast wall of metal that was getting wider every second. A huge wave girdling it was advancing towards us relentlessly. Richard Parker finally sensed the looming juggernaut. He turned and went 'Woof! Woof!' but not doglike — it was tigerlike: powerful, scary and utterly suited to the situation.

'Richard Parker, it's going to run us over! What are we going to do? Quick, quick, a flare! No! Must row. Oar in oarlock ... there! *HUMPF! HUMPF! HUMPF! HUMPF! HUMPF! HUM–*'

The bow wave pushed us up. Richard Parker crouched, and the hairs on him stood up. The lifeboat slid off the bow wave and missed the tanker by less than two feet.

The ship slid by for what seemed like a mile, a mile of high, black canyon wall, a mile of castle fortification with not a single sentinel to notice us languishing in the moat. I fired off a rocket flare, but I aimed it poorly. Instead of surging over the bulwarks and exploding in the captain's face, it ricocheted off the ship's side and went straight into the Pacific, where it died with a hiss. I blew my whistle with all my might. I shouted at the top of my lungs. All to no avail.

Its engines rumbling loudly and its propellers chopping explosively underwater, the ship churned past us and left us bouncing and bobbing in its frothy wake. After so many weeks of natural sounds, these mechanical noises were strange and awesome and stunned me into silence.

In less than twenty minutes a ship of three hundred thousand tons became a speck on the horizon. When I turned away, Richard Parker was still looking in its direction. After a few seconds he turned away too and our gazes briefly met. My eyes expressed longing, hurt, anguish, loneliness. All he was aware of was that something stressful and momentous had happened, something beyond the outer limits of his understanding. He did not see that it was salvation barely missed. He only saw that the alpha here, this odd, unpredictable tiger, had been very excited. He settled down to another nap. His sole comment on the event was a cranky miaow.

'I love you!' The words burst out pure and unfettered, infinite. The feeling flooded my chest. 'Truly I do. I love you, Richard Parker. If I didn't have you now, I don't know what I would do. I don't think I would make it. No, I wouldn't. I would die of hopelessness. Don't give up, Richard Parker, don't give up. I'll get you to land, I promise, I promise!'

(b) Read the extract again. Put the statements in the order in which they occur in the extract.

a　Pi starts to row the lifeboat.　☐

b　Pi realises that he has positive feelings about the tiger.　☐

c　Pi fires a flare but it isn't seen.　☐

d　Pi realises that the tanker might be going to hit the lifeboat.　[1]

e　Pi blows a whistle and shouts but no one hears him.　☐

f　The tanker disappears out of sight.　☐

g　Pi thinks that Richard Parker sees him as a kind of tiger.　☐

h　The noise of the tanker is strange to Pi after weeks at sea.　☐

i　The tiger goes to sleep.　☐

j　The wave of the tanker lifts the lifeboat up.　☐

c Replace the words in italics with a word or phrase from the box. Use the text to check the meanings of the words in the box.

> to no avail relentlessly speck looming anguish crouched with all his might languishing

1 I trudged on *in an extreme way* through the heavy rain to get back to our warm camp.

2 The *large and frightening* shape of the oncoming ship was clearly visible to us all.

3 We *bent our knees and lowered our body* behind a tree and kept quiet hoping not to be found.

4 The sick man had been *existing in an unpleasant situation* in a tent in the desert for almost a month.

5 Joseph tried *as hard as he could* to move the fallen tree from the road.

6 We advised Paula and George not to travel when they felt so ill, but it was *with no success at all*.

7 Helen's house is so clean; there isn't a *tiny spot* of dirt anywhere!

8 In Josie's *extreme unhappiness*, she forgot her suitcase when she left for the airport.

d Answer the questions.

1 Why do you think the tiger has not eaten the boy?

2 Why do you think the tanker didn't stop and help them?

3 Why do you think Pi says 'I love you, Richard Parker'?

8 Write

a Read the title of the composition in Exercise 8b and make a list of the arguments you expect to see.

b Read the composition quickly and check your answers. Which of the statements do you agree with?

c Work with a partner and discuss the questions.

1 How effective do you think the use of the dilemma in the introduction is? What other attention-grabbing ways of introducing the topic can you think of?

2 Underline the expressions the writer uses to try and present a balance of opinions.

3 How does the writer order the paragraphs?

d Choose a title from 1–5 and write a composition.

1 Should there be an international ban on animal testing?

2 Do zoos still have a place in today's world?

3 Should pet owners have to pay a licence?

4 National parks for animals, or land for people – which is more important?

5 Is violence sometimes caused by imitation of the violence in video games or on TV?

Should there be an international ban on animal testing?

Imagine the following scenario. You are, and have been for many years now, a staunch defender of animal rights. Clearly you are firmly against any kind of animal experimentation for scientific research. Then one day your doctor tells you that unless you undergo an immediate heart transplant, you will die. They perform a successful operation and you are given plenty more years of healthy living. How do you feel knowing that you are only alive because of a technology that was developed through extensive use of animal experimentation?

This, of course, is perhaps the most convincing argument in defence of the use of animals in scientific research and it is,

clearly, a hard one to refute. Even if we are not so unlucky as to need such major surgery, we all reap the benefits of medical advances. Most of these would take years longer or even never happen at all if it was not for animal testing. It is very easy to stand up and criticise the scientists for conducting their tests on monkeys and rats without really taking into consideration how much their work does to improve the qualities of our lives.

On the other hand, animals are living creatures and undeniably have their own rights to life. They are, unfortunately, far too often used in research that is completely unnecessary and does nothing for the general good of mankind. I include in this

category, cosmetic products and cigarettes. I believe it is becoming more and more difficult to defend this practice. However, there are still plenty of people who would like to see a veto on all animal cruelty.

There is no doubt that this is a complex issue and it has divided both scientific and public opinion for many years now. Indeed it is probably one of the most controversial issues of our times. Perhaps because there are so many convincing arguments on both sides, I find it hard to know exactly where my own feelings lie. Although I could clearly support a stop to pointless testing, I am not sure if I could go along with a total ban.

For your portfolio

10 The sporting spirit

* could / be able to / manage to
* Vocabulary: success and failure

1 Read and listen

a Look at the photographs and answer the questions.

1 Which sport is involved in each one?
2 Which of the sports do you think requires the most determination?
3 What qualities do you think are needed to be a good sportsman/ sportswoman?

b Read the three texts quickly. Which text mentions these things? There may be more than one text.

1 finishing an event	5 the reaction of spectators
2 not finishing an event	6 the reaction of newspapers
3 the reaction of team-mates	7 injuries
4 the reaction of an opponent	8 an apology

(1)

Rower suffers backlash

An Australian rower ^A_____ has endured a media battering. With 400 metres remaining in the 2004 Olympic Games women's eight final, 23-year-old Sally Robbins suddenly quit, to the astonishment of her team-mates and sport-mad country. Robbins slumped in her boat and stopped rowing. Australia finished last.

Robbins blamed her collapse on exhaustion after the gruelling first 1600 metres of the race on the hottest day of the year in Athens. She also revealed that her team-mates had threatened to throw her into the water.

'I didn't say anything because I was stunned myself,' Robbins said. 'Fatigue set in and I just couldn't move,' she added. 'It's a feeling of paralysis ^B_____ .'

But certain sections of the Australian media and her own team-mates criticised her actions. The Australian press contrasted Robbins' actions with Grant Hackett, Australia's swimming hero, who managed to win the 1500 metres gold medal despite a partially collapsed lung. 'His was real heroism – he did everything it took to fulfil his ambition,' said an editorial.

On a television show, another member of the team indicated that she had expected Robbins to collapse because she had suffered from similar problems at the 2002 World Championships. She also said she would not want to row with Robbins again for some time.

Robbins said that she might be able to row in the team again in the future.

'It'll be a long process, but I think I'll be back eventually,' she said. 'Obviously I have to ^C_____ .'

Whether she will be able to get that trust back remains to be seen.

(2)

Magnificently last

Yesterday, 20 October, 1968. The place: Olympic Stadium, Mexico City. The time: 7.00pm. The closing ceremonies had just been completed. The spectators were gathering their belongings to leave the stadium. Then the announcer asked them to remain in their seats, because the last runner in the men's marathon – the final event of the Olympics – was about to come into the stadium.

The crowd were confused. The marathon had finished hours before; the medals had already been awarded. What had taken this man so long? The question was answered when the runner appeared. John Akhwari, from Tanzania, had fallen early in the race: he had hit his head on the road, cut and damaged his knee, and yet, 40 kilometres later, he was staggering to the finishing line.

The response of the crowd was overwhelming. They gave Akhwari a standing ovation that far exceeded the one given the man ^D_____ . Akhwari managed to cross the finishing line, but then he collapsed and was immediately rushed to hospital.

Akhwari appeared before sports journalists to answer questions about his extraordinary feat. The first question was obvious: 'Why, with those injuries, did you run to the end, when you couldn't possibly win a medal?' Akhwari's reply was: ^E_____ . My country didn't send me over 11,000 kilometres to start the race. They sent me here to finish it.'

Punishments handed out

Ten minutes from the end of the 2006 World Cup final, Zinedine Zidane and Marco Materazzi exchanged words as the two walked upfield. Zidane appeared to be walking away from the Italian, but then turned, lowered his head and butted Materazzi in the chest, F_____ . Zidane was sent off. Materazzi was hurt but was able to play on, and Italy went on to win their fourth World Cup, 5–3 on penalties after a 1–1 extra-time draw.

Zidane had to G_____ as punishment for the head butt. The French player, voted the best player in the championship, was originally fined $6,000 by FIFA and given a three-match suspension. However, the suspension could not be applied since Zidane retired from football immediately after the game, so he agreed to work with children instead. Materazzi was suspended for two games and fined $4,000.

Zidane said that he had attacked Materazzi because of insults to members of his family. FIFA said that Materazzi had been suspended for 'repeatedly provoking Zidane'.

Both players apologised to FIFA for their inappropriate behaviour and expressed their regret at the incident. In an appearance on French television, Zidane also apologised H_____ to younger players.

(3)

(c) 🔊 Fill in the spaces A–H in the texts with phrases 1–8. Then listen to check.

1. knocking him to the ground
2. do community service
3. who suffered a mid-race collapse
4. who, hours before, had come in first
5. for setting a bad example
6. I don't think you understand
7. where you just hit the wall
8. earn their trust

Discussion box

Work in pairs or small groups. Discuss these questions together.

1. Which of the sportspeople in the texts acted badly or well? Give reasons for your opinions.
2. Do people in sport have a responsibility to act in certain ways and set examples for others?
3. Are there any other incidents/stories from sport which have made an impression on you? Tell the class.

2 Grammar

could / be able to / manage to

(a) **Read the examples and then complete the rules with the words in the box.**

> modal verbs   general   ability
> specific   non-ability

Rules:

- We can use *could /couldn't* to talk about _____ ability in the past, for example:
  When I was a kid, I could stand on my head but I couldn't swim.
  After a month in China, I could understand some Chinese but I couldn't speak a word.
- When we talk about ability at _____ moments in the past, we can use *couldn't* or *wasn't able to* for _____ , but we have to use *be able to* or *manage to* for _____ , for example:
  *Fatigue set in and I just **couldn't move**.* or *I just **wasn't able to move**.*
  *He was hurt but he **was able to play** on. (not 'could play')*
  *He **managed to cross** the finishing line but then he collapsed. (not 'could cross')*
- We use *managed to* for things we were able to do, but with some difficulty.
- When we talk about ability with other _____ or auxiliaries, we have to use *be able to*, for example:
  *She said that she **might be able to row** in the team again in the future.*
  *Whether she **will be able to get** that trust back remains to be seen.*

(b) **Complete each sentence. There may be more than one possibility.**

1. I was so scared that I *couldn't / wasn't able to* move.
2. We had to stand in the queue for hours but we _____ get tickets in the end.
3. They had more than twenty shots at goal but _____ score – so we won 1–0!
4. I tried to play tennis for the first time yesterday, but I only _____ hit the ball once!
5. He hurt his ankle and he hasn't _____ play football for two weeks.
6. Thanks for the invitation to your party next week, but I'm afraid I won't _____ come.
7. My parents told me that I _____ walk when I was only ten months old.
8. There are lots of good shops in the town, so you should _____ find what you want.

3 Listen

(a) What do both of the photos show? What, if anything, do they have in common?

(b) 🔊 Listen to the conversation between Paul and Jenny and answer the questions.

1 Which sports do they mention during the conversation?
2 Which of these topics best represents the topic of their conversation?
 a Sportspeople should try to win at any cost.
 b Cheating in sport is inevitable.
 c Cheating in sport may or may not be acceptable.

(c) 🔊 Listen again. Write J (Jenny) or P (Paul) in the boxes to show who expresses these ideas.

1 Winning is the most important thing. ☐
2 All teams try to win and this may involve breaking the rules. ☐
3 Illegal actions in sport are the worst part of the game. ☐
4 It's basically impossible for sportsmen/sportswomen to admit to illegal actions. ☐
5 There's a difference between cheating and disagreeing. ☐
6 Sport can be enjoyable despite some instances of cheating. ☐

(d) 🔊 Listen again. Complete the sentences from the conversation with the words from the box.

advantage   dived   fairly   shout   intentionally

1 But our player .... – he was trying to get a penalty.
2 I just wish we'd won ...., I suppose.
3 What I'd like them to do is not to handle the ball .... in the first place.
4 I mean, tennis players get angry and .... at the referee sometimes, don't they?
5 Cheating ..., it's doing something that you know isn't allowed, in order to gain an ....

(e) Write ✓ (yes) or ✗ (no) in the boxes to indicate your opinions. Compare your view with others in the class.

1 I mostly agree with Jenny. ☐
2 I mostly agree with Paul. ☐
3 I don't agree with either of them. ☐

Discussion box

Work in pairs or small groups. Discuss these questions together.

1 Do you agree with Paul that cheating generally occurs in team sports? Give examples.
2 Do you believe psychological tactics (for example diving to get a penalty, or toilet breaks in tennis) are increasing in today's world of sport? Why / why not?
3 Do you think there is anything that referees and umpires can do to decrease cheating in sport? Are there any ways in which technology might help them?

4 Vocabulary

Success and failure

a Read the sentences. Put the underlined verbs (in infinitive form) into the correct column in the table.

1 He hasn't got any money, so it looks like his plan to start a business will fall through.
2 She was very shy as a child, but she overcame it and now she's really sociable.
3 I thought it would be impossible for him, but he pulled it off.
4 I had an interview for the job but I blew it, so I have to start looking again.
5 I did a film test, but I messed it up so I don't think I'll get the part.
6 The course was great! It fulfilled all my expectations.
7 He's very ambitious and he works hard – I think he'll make it to the top.
8 It's very easy to use a computer – you can't go wrong!

having a positive result	having a negative result
to succeed	to fail

b Circle the correct words.

1 I followed the map, but I *went wrong* / *made it* somewhere and got lost.
2 This is a great chance for you – make sure you don't *blow it* / *pull it off*.
3 Congratulations! I didn't think you could do it, but you *made it* / *overcame it* in the end.
4 My plans worked well at the start, but in the end they *fell through* / *made it*.
5 No one has ever managed to do this – so I don't think you can *pull it off* / *blow it*, either.
6 Everyone has problems – you just have to *fulfil* / *overcome* them.
7 She's got lots of talent and promise for the future – I hope she *fulfils* / *overcomes* it.
8 I'm sure I won't pass – I really *fell through* / *messed up* the exam.

c Complete the sentences with the missing words.

1 When was the last time you really messed _____ an exam and what exactly _____ wrong?
2 When was the last time you had a plan fall _____ and what was it?
3 What do you need to do if you want to _____ it as a politician in your country?
4 What problems will you have to _____ if you want to succeed in your chosen career?

d Work with a partner. Choose two of the questions from Exercise 4c and talk about them.

5 Read and speak

a Complete the sentences with the quotations from sportspeople in the box.

> play together   can't win   come second
> win or lose   get it right
> take the game-winning shot

1 'You may have the greatest bunch of individual stars in the world, but if they don't _____ , the club won't be worth a dime.' (Babe Ruth, baseball player)
2 'I've missed more than 9000 shots in my career. I've lost almost 300 games. 26 times, I've been trusted to _____ and missed. I've failed over and over again. And that's why I succeed.' (Michael Jordan, basketball player)
3 'If you're first, you're first. If you _____ , you're nothing.' (Bill Shankly, football manager)
4 'Champions keep playing until they _____ .' (Billie Jean King, tennis player)
5 'If you _____ , make the one ahead of you break the record.' (Jan McKeithen, athlete)
6 'Whoever said "It's not whether you _____ that counts," probably lost.' (Martina Navratilova, tennis player)

b Work with a partner. Discuss the questions.

1 Which of the quotes in Exercise 5a can you most/least relate to and why?
2 Which of the quotes are relevant for life in general? Explain why.

c Work with a partner and use your ideas to complete the sentences.

1 Life without sports is like ...
2 Being second is not as good as coming first, but ...
3 Champions aren't made in the gym. Champions are ...
4 Football is a wonderful way of ...

Speaking

6 Listen and speak

a 🔊 Listen to Marco giving a short presentation to his class about the city of Brasília. Number the pictures in the order Marco mentions them.

a ☐

c ☐

d ☐

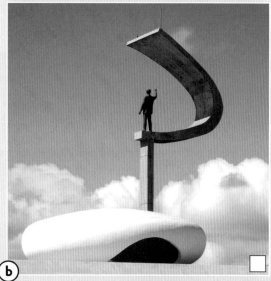

b ☐

b 🔊 Listen again and tick (✓) the phrases as you hear them.

1 Anyway, ...   ☐
2 as it happens ...   ☐
3 by the way, ...   ☐
4 bear with me for a moment?   ☐
5 in fact, ...   ☐
6 To sum up, ...   ☐
7 just as a matter of interest, ...   ☐
8 Now the first thing I want to say, ...   ☐
9 Now, ...   ☐
10 Right – going back to ...   ☐

c Write the number in the boxes of the phrase or phrases 1–10 in Exercise 6b that Marco uses to:

- begin his talk ☐
- end his talk ☐
- to return to something he was saying before ☐
- begin a new point ☐
- give himself time to think ☐
- add an extra point to what he is saying ☐
- emphasise something he was saying ☐

d Prepare to give a short talk on one of the subjects in the box to your class. The talk should be one or two minutes.

> a famous town   a famous person
> a famous team   a famous building

Make notes but do not write down exactly what you're going to say. Use phrases from Exercise 6b to help your listeners follow what you say.

e Give your talk to others in your class.

7 Pronunciation

Linking sounds

🔊 Turn to page 122.

8 Write

a Read the report quickly and answer the questions.

1. Which sport is involved?
2. Is this Newhaven or Shorthouse's school magazine? Why do you think so?

LAST GASP WINNER

Last week's match between Newhaven and Shorthouse was one of the most closely fought affairs to have been seen for many years. We had expected a competitive match, but few of us could have imagined anything quite like this.

The first fifteen minutes were comparatively slow, with each team sizing up the other. A heavy tackle by the Shorthouse captain on Lewis, however, warmed things up and after that the game became much more open and exciting.

However, scoring chances were few and far between until the 28th minute when the Shorthouse centre forward broke through – all he had to do was put the ball in the net, but incredibly he put the ball over the bar. About five minutes later, almost the same thing happened again but this time the player made no mistake, 1–0 to Shorthouse and it stayed that way until half-time.

Who knows what Mr Ackroyd said to the Newhaven players during the interval, but it certainly made a difference since the home side came out on the attack in the second half. Only five minutes had gone by when Lewis picked up a loose ball, slipped past the last Shorthouse player and smashed in the equaliser. The rest of the second half was non-stop attacking, with both teams going close on several occasions. However it was only in the last minute that Newhaven sealed their win – Jameson went past the goalkeeper, who brought him down and the referee had no hesitation in awarding the penalty. The Shorthouse players complained bitterly, but there was no doubt in anyone else's mind that it was a penalty, and Jameson himself coolly scored from the spot for a thoroughly deserved 2–1 win.

b Match the underlined words and phrases in the text with their meanings 1–8.

1. continuous *non-stop*
2. without anxiety
3. rare
4. strongly and in an angry way
5. completed
6. missed
7. measuring
8. scored

c What is the effect of using the underlined words in the text instead of the expressions in Exercise 8b?

d Write a description of one of the three events. Write 200–250 words.

- a sports event that you remember well
- a musical event that you remember well
- an event on the streets of your town that you remember well (for example, a parade or a demonstration)

Think about these questions before you write:
- When did you experience the event?
- Where did it take place?
- Who were you with?
- What made it so memorable for you?
- How many verbs, adjectives and adverbs can you use to make it as lively and dramatic as possible?

For your portfolio

Superheroes

* Negative inversions
* Vocabulary: from human to hero

1 Read and listen

(a) How many of the superheroes on this page do you recognise? What do you know about them? Think about their powers, their mission in life, their personalities and who their enemies/friends are.

(b) Read the text quickly and check your answers to Exercise 1a.

SUPERHEROES

Have you got what it takes?

[1] Not only are they forced to live their lives in solitude but they also have to change their clothes in dirty old phone booths. Then they have to keep their true identities a secret and therefore find it difficult to hang on to any meaningful relationship. They face life-threatening situations on a daily basis and are then often criticised for their heroics by an unappreciative world. So who on earth would want to be a superhero anyway?

[2] Everyone, so it would seem, according to the creators of *Who wants to be a superhero?*, a TV reality show that started a few years ago in the US and proved to be an instant hit with television audiences. And who was one of those creators? None other than Stan Lee – yes, the very same Mr Lee who created Spider-Man and The Incredible Hulk all those years ago. If anyone knows anything about superheroes, then Stan Lee would be that man.

[3] The show featured eleven ordinary contestants who thought they had what it takes to become a superhero. Each contestant had to come up with an original idea for a superhero, complete with a name, their own costume and their best superhero attitude. Each week the contestants were tested on a variety of superhero qualities, and each week, two contestants were eliminated. But there had to be a twist somewhere and in this case, it was the obvious need for an evil foe. After all, no superhero would be complete without an arch-enemy, so it was up to Mr Lee to convert one of the hero hopefuls over to the Dark Side.

[4] Sound silly? Of course. Grown-ups running around in tights and a cape could be nothing else, but that's exactly what made it so much fun. Deep down inside each of us, they say, is the desire to be a superhero. But just what exactly are the qualities you would need to be one?

[5] Well, rarely do you find a superhero without some kind of supernatural ability. Being able to see through walls (like Superman) or spin webs out of your fingers (like Spider-Man) are quite useful, after all. Phenomenal strength comes in handy too – though in the case of The Incredible Hulk, it was a bit of a problem since he only acquired the strength when he was really angry, which led to a tendency to smash things up a bit (not to mention the need for a new set of clothes every time he went back to normal). Speed's good too – Superman had this, of course (well, what was just a bit boring about him was that he had all the abilities, really – the same goes for Wonder Woman) – and flying is high on the list as well: Superman, Spider-Man, the Incredibles, and many others too. As for the X-men: between them, they had all the supernatural abilities you could wish for.

[6] But to qualify as a superhero, you need other, more human qualities too. The desire to do good is probably number one on the list. Saving people from burning buildings; stopping powerful bank robbers or international masterminds; generally, helping the honest, ordinary people against whatever evils happen to be around. Courage is important too – the courage to do what's right even if it means you're putting yourself in great danger makes a fairly frequent appearance in superhero stories.

[7] Strange though it might sound, another typical human quality of superheroes is weakness – a touch of frailty, of human weakness, is essential, crucial even. You see, a superhero must present to the reader an image with which he or she can associate. That's why they have always been constructed so as to be recognisable as human beings. Superheroes have a home, or at least a setting and other people that they are attached to: colleagues, friends, a parental influence that makes them more understandable and sympathetic to readers.

[8] This explains why most superheroes have been given a double identity. Because since the hero in uniform becomes too perfect to have any human frailties (and therefore becomes a bit remote from us mortals), he or she has another side, a much more human and understandable one, so that the readers can know him or her better. In uniform, Superman is far too perfect for anyone to associate with him directly. But as Clark Kent, a short-sighted, shy, nervous guy who can't even find a way to invite Lois Lane out on a date, the readers or viewers can see themselves, and enjoy a little daily make-believe that they, too, are really superheroes.

c 🔊 Read the text again and listen. (Circle) the correct answers a, b or c.

1 Which of these points does the author *not* raise about the life of a superhero in the introduction?
   a They find it difficult to make good friends.
   b No matter how hard they work, their job is never done.
   c They're sometimes misunderstood by the general public.
   d They have to lead double lives.

2 Which of the following points is *not* mentioned about the TV show *Who wants to be a superhero?*
   a A lot of people liked the programme.
   b Two of the contestants were thrown off the show each week.
   c Each programme was introduced by Stan Lee.
   d One of the contestants was changed into a super villain.

3 Which of these typical physical abilities of a superhero is *not* mentioned?
   a Being able to jump great distances
   b X-ray vision
   c Being incredibly strong
   d Being fast

4 According to the text, what is the most important human quality a superhero should have?
   a They should always want to make the world a better place.
   b They should be brave.
   c They should be honest.
   d They should have the ability to question their decisions.

5 Why is it so important that superheroes should have a weakness?
   a To make the stories more interesting.
   b So they can lead double lives.
   c So we can identify with them more easily.
   d To make them less perfect.

d Find expressions in the text which could be replaced with the following words and phrases.

1 very dangerous (paragraph 1)
2 every day (paragraph 1)
3 an immediate success (paragraph 2)
4 defeated in a competition (paragraph 3)
5 enemy (paragraph 3)
6 is useful (paragraph 5)
7 break things violently (paragraph 5)
8 doesn't know how to (paragraph 8)
9 pretence (paragraph 8)

Discussion box

Work in pairs or small groups. Discuss these questions together.

1 Why do you think superheroes (and particularly films about them) are so popular?
2 When do you think an interest in superheroes becomes an obsession?
3 Why might we need superheroes in our modern world?
4 Which real people do you think deserve the title of superhero or super heroine?

2 Grammar

Negative inversions

a) Look at the examples from the text. <u>Underline</u> the correct option to complete the rule.

Not only are they forced to live their lives in solitude but they also have to change their clothes in dirty old phone booths.

Rarely do you find a superhero without some kind of supernatural ability

Rule:

• We can bring *positive/negative* adverbs and adverbial phrases to the *beginning/end* of a sentence to make it *more/less* emphatic. If we do this then the rest of the sentence follows the pattern of a *normal statement/ question*. This is much more commonly found in *written/spoken* English. Some of the adverbs and adverbial phrases commonly used include: *never, rarely, not only … but also, under no circumstances, on no account, no sooner … than*

b) (Circle) the correct answer in each statement.

1   Never *action films have / have action films* been so popular.

2   *You will / Will you* rarely see such a disappointing film.

3   On no account *you should / should you* leave the cinema before this film has finished.

4   No sooner *the opening credits had / had the opening credits* finished than I wanted to walk out of the cinema.

5   Under no circumstances *I can / can I* recommend this film.

6   *It's / Is it* not only great fun for kids but there's something in it for adults too.

7   *I have / Have I* never been so bored in my life.

8   Not only *he directed / did he direct* the film, but he wrote it too.

c) Rewrite the sentences using the word in brackets at the beginning of the sentence.

1   Just as Batman's finished fighting one enemy, another one appears. (No sooner … than)

   No sooner has Batman finished fighting one enemy than another one appears.

2   You should not touch that under any circumstances. (Under no circumstances)

3   I have never read such rubbish before. (Never)

4   Superman can see through walls and he can fly. (Not only … but also)

5   You will rarely see such great special effects as in the new Superman film. (Rarely)

6   You must not say a word to anyone. (On no account)

7   My friend looks just like Clark Kent and he's a journalist. (Not only … but also)

8   I'd just sat down to watch the film when the phone rang. (No sooner … than)

3 Vocabulary

From human to hero

Complete the captions with the words in the box.

> slouched   panted   puny   superhuman strength   short-sighted
> speed of light   squinted   X-ray vision   short of breath

Before the radioactive snake bit him, Jack was just an everyday kid.

He was ¹ _____ and ² _____ when he read.

He was ³ _____ and ⁴ _____ when he walked.

He was always ⁵ _____ and he ⁶ _____ when he ran.

Now, Jack is the Cobra …

Now he has ⁷ _____ .

He has ⁸ _____ .

He can fly at the ⁹ _____ .

4 Listen

(a) Look at pictures 1–3 and decide on a name for each of the would-be superheroes.

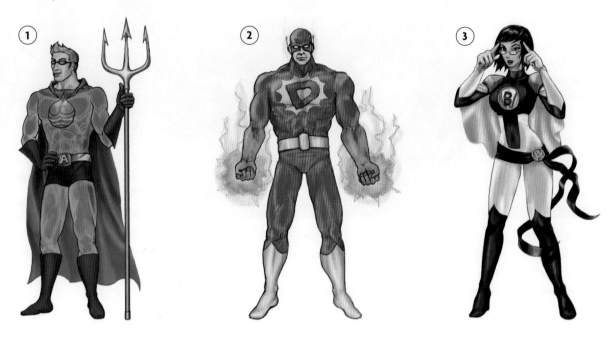

(1)   (2)   (3)

(b) 🔊 Listen to the auditions for a TV reality show *Have you got what it takes to save the world?* and complete the first two columns in the table.

(c) 🔊 Listen again and complete the table.

Name	Special powers	Weaknesses	Mission	Arch-enemy
1				
2				
3				

(d) Which superhero from Exercise 4c do you think should get a part on the show?

5 Speak

Saving the day

(a) Work in a group of three. Read the task sheet and create your team.

The world is facing danger like it has never seen before. A group of super villains are threatening to destroy life as we know it:

- The Generator has plans to steal all the earth's natural resources to power his huge army of automated robots.
- Tedium wants to take over the world's media and use it to control the minds of all of us.
- Seemingly respectable Politico is running for world presidency, a position he will use to bring war and destruction to the whole planet.

Your task is to design a group of superheroes known collectively as The Fabulous Three. Between them they must be able to take on and defeat these villains. Each of your superheroes should have a name and special powers to help them save the world.

(b) Present your team to the rest of the class. Vote on which team will get the job.

Culture in mind

6 Read

(a) Read the texts quickly and match the superheroes 1–4 with their pictures.

1   Jalila
2   Nagraj
3   Rakan
4   Captain Canuck

It's not just American superheroes who patrol the world. There are hundreds of other superheroes from many countries all over the globe. Here are just a few.

In February 2004, Egypt-based AK Comics became the Middle East's first producer of superhero comic books when they launched several titles in both Arabic and English. The aim of the publishing house was: 'to fill the cultural gap created over the years by providing essentially Arab role models, in our case, Arab superheroes, to become a source of pride to our young generations.'

AK Comics have four superheroes: Rakan, Zein, Jalila and Aya. Rakan is a medieval warrior who was raised by a sabre-tooth tiger and lives in an ancient world of sword and sorcery. The others are all based in a near future shortly after of the 55-year war. Zein, a descendant of the pharaohs, is a professor of philosophy. Aya is a law student who fights (without the use of any special powers) for justice and Jalila is a scientist who gained her super-powers when she survived an explosion at a nuclear plant.

The comics sell mainly in Egypt but are also beginning to be distributed in other parts of the world. There are also plans to give the characters their own animated cartoon series.

It's 1993 and Canada is the most powerful country in the world. But it will only remain this way so long as Captain Canuck continues to patrol the borders and keep harm at bay. Captain Canuck, who first appeared in 1975, is one of Canada's most popular superheroes and proudly wears the familiar maple leaf symbol on his forehead. There have actually been three different Canucks, each of them a government agent. The first was Tom Evans, who gained his superhuman strength after an encounter with aliens. He was followed by Richard Comely who fought a huge global conspiracy. Finally there was David Semple, a constable in the famous Canadian Mounties, who put on the costume to do battle with a biker gang. Each incarnation was drawn and written by a different team. In the future, his mission will be to stop illegal arms from reaching his homeland.

By day, Raj is a public relations officer for the fictitious Bharti Communications Company. He is quite shy and unassuming and he is also terrified of snakes (or so he pretends). But at the first sign of trouble Raj is transformed into Nagraj (Snakeman), perhaps the most popular superhero from India's famous Raj Comics.

The idea behind Nagraj's character is heavily influenced by the Hindu myth of the shape-shifting snake. His power comes from the millions of microscopic snakes that live in his blood. These give him superhuman strength, a poisonous bite and the ability to heal. He can also shoot snakes out of his wrists and change into a snake whenever he wants.

Nagraj's secret identity, Raj, was a later development, but many hardcore fans will argue it was an unnecessary one. In the early days of his conception, (he was created in the late 1980s) Nagraj battled international terrorism all over the world, although he actually started out as a weapon for the terrorists. More recently, Nagraj's enemies are of a more fantastical nature and the storylines often involve the world of magic and time travel.

(b) Read the texts again. Which superhero:

1   has been brought to life by more than one man?
2   was brought up by an animal which is now extinct?
3   has an ancient and royal background?
4   doesn't actually have any special abilities?
5   once worked for the people he then went on to fight?
6   is a patriotic defender of his country?

Discussion box

Work in pairs or small groups. Discuss these questions together.

1   What superheroes are there specifically from your country?
2   Why is it important for countries to have their own superheroes?

7 Write

a Work with a partner. The words in the box are connected to films. What do they mean?

> series   special effects   sequel   action   star   characters   plot   scene

A series is a collection of two or more films that follow the same characters.

b Read the film review of *X-men: The Last Stand* and complete it with the words in Exercise 7a. Can you find an example of a negative inversion?

X-MEN: THE LAST STAND

Rarely are part twos as good as the original film. So when it comes to part threes, I suppose there's even less hope. *X-men III* promised to be different. After all, *X-Men II* is regarded by many fans as one of the best comic book movies ever made. However, this ¹_____ , although exciting at times, is ultimately uninspiring, despite a ²_____ which deals with the invention of a controversial cure for the mutants. Considering the amount of action and life-changing events which occur in *X-Men: The Last Stand*, you'd expect to feel more moved. But this third film outing for the mutant superheroes and villains is surprisingly short of real emotion.

As in the previous movies, Hugh Jackman is the highlight. His Wolverine coming across like a young Clint Eastwood, with huge metal claws, is easily the best bit of the film. There's talk of a ³_____ of films just for Wolverine in the future and it's not surprising: he's easily the most engaging character. The real ⁴_____ should be Famke Janssen, whose Jean Grey returns from a watery grave as the world-threatening Dark Phoenix in a spectacular ⁵_____ . It's a pity that her heart and soul are rather lost beneath the computer generated ⁶_____ _____ .

Of the other ⁷_____ , Halle Berry's Storm is boring, Kelsey Grammer is given little to work with as Beast, and none of the youngsters make an impression. If you're a fan of the first two movies then you'll probably feel a little disappointed as the ⁸_____ skips through events so swiftly, there's no time to get to know any of the characters. There's some satisfaction from watching the mutant story reach a kind of conclusion, although I'm sure they'll be back for more. Jackman and Janssen are too good for the film to be totally unwatchable, but unless you're already dedicated to the X-Men, *The Last Stand* won't really hold up.

c Read the review again and answer the questions.

1 Which one word would you use to sum up the critic's overall opinion of the film?
2 What did he find to like about the film?
3 What are his main criticisms of the film?
4 What outside information does he give about the film?

d Find the following expressions in the review. Does the reviewer use them in conjunction with a positive or negative point?

1 Considering the ... you'd expect ...
2 ... is surprisingly short on ...
3 ... is the highlight ...
4 ... is easily the best bit ...
5 It's a pity that ...
6 If you're a fan of ... you'll probably feel a bit ...
7 There's some satisfaction from ...
8 ... won't really hold up.

e Write a review of a film that you found disappointing. Try and include each point in the table.

Content	Language
A short synopsis of the plot (not too long)	One example of a negative inversion. Look at Exercise 2 for some ideas.
The reasons why you found the film disappointing	Some of the film words from Exercise 7a
A few positive points (if possible)	Some of the expressions from Exercise 7d

On your own

* Mixed conditional review
* Alternatives to *if*
* Vocabulary: more time expressions

1 Read and listen

(a) Look at the picture. Where is he and what do you think he is doing? Read the introduction and check your ideas.

Canadian Bob Kull had an idea for his PhD degree. He wanted to study the physical, emotional and spiritual effects of deep wilderness solitude. He decided the best way to do this was to make himself the test subject. He decided to spend a year living on a remote island off the coast of Chile. He travelled to Chile, prepared the equipment, materials, and supplies he would need for a year alone in the wilderness, and went to a tiny remote island on Chile's extreme southern coast, ten hours by sea from the nearest settlement. It would be his home for the next year, and apart from seeing people only once, he spent his time completely on his own.

(b) How do you think he filled his time there? Predict five things you think he did.

(c) Read the diary extracts quickly and check your ideas.

Island diary

June

[1] I have been here for four and a half months now, and until a couple of days ago the solitude was complete. I often think I hear human sounds, but it is always the wind in the trees or the sea crashing among the rocks. I also frequently think I hear the sound of a motor, but it turns out to be the kettle boiling, or the wind generator humming, A_____ or the roar of a distant waterfall. But a couple of days ago the sound I heard really was a motor. The man from the National Park Service B_____ came by. He lives in the neighbouring park. There are four employees for this area of islands and peninsulas and fjords. Other than myself, there is simply no one else here. But it feels so natural to be here that I don't often think about the solitude unless I stop to remember and reflect on how truly fortunate I am to be able to be here like this. If I had never come here, I wouldn't know how valuable solitude is.

[2] So I had company for a while. The ranger and his three assistants dropped in to see my set-up. They liked what I've built and said they hoped it would still be here after I've left. C_____ . It would be much easier for me to leave it, and after all the work building it, I sort of hate to tear it back down. But I would like to leave the area as much like I found it as possible when I go. D_____ . When my visitors were ready to leave, I was ready too. I was, surprisingly, happy enough to have the company for a while, and was also happy to be on my own again once they had gone.

December

[3] Long ago I put away my watch. At the beginning of November I put away the barometer, thermometer and tide tables E_____ . For the most part I have stopped reading and writing – laptop and books hidden away, and over and over when I catch myself at it, I let go of useless repetitive thinking, fruitless planning, and idle speculation. Coming back to my own direct experience of the here and now: to my body and heart and mind. To the question, 'Who am I?'

[4] All the physical work is done until it is time to take down the shelter in February. Since early October there have only been four or five days calm enough to fish from the kayak so mostly I am land-bound F_____ . I can wander perhaps 150 metres along the rocky coast. If the rain forest behind me wasn't so dense, I'm sure I'd have explored more of it. G_____

[5] When I do go fishing, I feel more and more deeply the life I take in killing the fish. My emotions are ambivalent: I feel a deep connection, gratitude and appreciation for the gift of sustenance from the sea and also sorrow H_____ in taking the life of one of my fellow creatures. Yet out here alone, I see death daily and know that all beings survive by ending the lives of others. There is underlying harmony and oneness in our common existence, we are all alive together here, yet there is also surface conflict; competition for food and space.

d 🔊 Read the text again and listen. Match the phrases 1–8 with spaces A–H in the text.

1   , and took down the wind generator
2   who is in charge of this whole huge area
3   But just getting into it is so difficult.
4   or a hummingbird making wind with its wings,
5   (and perhaps guilt and shame)
6   It is so undisturbed here.
7   on this small patch of earth
8   Hmmm. A dilemma …

e Read the text again. Which months did these things happen?

1   He arrived on the island.
2   He was visited by four men.
3   He packed away a lot of his possessions.
4   He took down his accommodation.

f Circle the best definition for each of the words from the text.

1   humming (paragraph 1) *making a low vibrating sound* / *not working properly* / *producing energy*
2   in charge of (paragraph 1) *owns* / *takes care of* / *is responsible for*
3   dropped by (paragraph 2) *made an informal visit* / *telephoned* / *arrived by air*
4   set up (paragraph 2) *research* / *living arrangements* / *official visa*
5   undisturbed (paragraph 2) *naturally beautiful* / *excited* / *untouched by humans*
6   wander (paragraph 4) *walk casually* / *swim* / *see*
7   dense (paragraph 4) *dangerous* / *dark* / *thick*
8   ambiguous (paragraph 5) *clear* / *exciting* / *confusing*

Discussion box

Work in pairs or small groups. Discuss these questions together.

1   How do you think Bob changed over the months?
2   How easy is it to get away from people completely in today's world? Where would you go to do an experiment like this and why?
3   How would you feel if you did an experiment like this?

2 Speak

Work with a partner. You have to spend one year alone on a desert island. There are a number of certain rules:

●   You can only take eight things.
●   You have to complete a project there.
●   You can only keep in contact with two people while you are there.
●   You need to raise money for your adventure before you go.

Talk about how you would fulfil each of the above rules. Then discuss what you would do and how you would survive the time there.

3 Grammar

Mixed conditionals review

a Look at the examples from the text. Match the examples with definitions i–ii.

1   *If the rain forest behind me wasn't so dense, I'm sure I'd have explored more of it.*
2   *If I had never come here, I wouldn't know how valuable solitude is.*

i   Describes the present consequence of a past action.
ii Describes how a general truth affects a past action.

b Rewrite the sentences using one of the mixed conditional patterns.

1   I feel lonely today because I didn't speak to anyone last night.
    If I had spoken to someone last night, I wouldn't be feeling lonely today.
2   I didn't catch any fish yesterday so I'm feeling hungry today.
3   I'm not a big reader so I didn't bring many books with me.
4   My camera is broken so I didn't take any photos yesterday.
5   I only know it's my birthday today because I brought a calendar with me.
6   My mouth is hurting because I pulled my tooth out yesterday.
7   My fishing rod is broken so I didn't go fishing this morning.
8   I'm a bit tired today because I didn't sleep well last night.

4 Listen

(a) Work in a small group. Look at the pictures of different activities. Think of one advantage and one disadvantage for doing each activity on your own.

 ① ☐  ② ☐  ③ ☐  ④ ☐

(b) 🔊 Listen to three teenagers talking about things they like doing on their own and things they like doing with other people. Tick (✓) the activities in Exercise 4a they talk about. What other activities do they talk about?

(c) 🔊 Listen again and complete sentences 1–8 with *Alex*, *Judy* or *Harry*.

1 .... needs to be able to stay in touch with people all the time.
2 .... would want to always go on holiday with other people.
3 .... thinks it's important to use time alone well.
4 .... could last about six hours without talking to anyone.
5 .... thinks you need time alone to work out problems.
6 .... uses time alone to make life plans.
7 .... can happily spend hours alone.
8 .... would find it extremely difficult to spend a whole day completely alone.

(d) Work with a partner. Talk about whether you are most like Harry, Judy or Alex. Explain why.

5 Vocabulary

More time expressions

(a) Read the sentences from the listening in Exercise 4. Circle the correct answer.

1 How do you *empty* / *fill* / *make* the time when you're alone?
2 ... it *makes* / *gives* / *gets* you time and space to think and sort things out a bit.
3 I'm *killing* / *murdering* / *assassinating* time until I see some of my friends again.
4 ... my mobile is an absolute must for me *at* / *in* / *on* all times.
5 In *neither* / *no* / *not* time at all I want to be together with someone else.
6 ... find yourself alone and with time on your *arms* / *hands* / *shoulders*.
7 I'm afraid our time's *in* / *out* / *up* for this week.

(b) Work with a partner. Where might you find notices 1–5?

① **Give us your washing and we'll give you time to do something better.**
....

② **FILL YOUR TIME THESE HOLIDAYS. COME AND WORK FOR US.**
....

③ Make time to give blood – you could be saving a life.
....

④ Time on your hands?
– come and help us to help the homeless.
....

⑤ Learn with us and you'll be speaking Spanish in no time at all.
....

(c) Replace the underlined expressions in Exercise 5b with a phrase from the box.

make it possible for you	find something to do
find the time	have you got nothing to do?
very quickly	

6 Grammar

Alternatives to *if*

a) Look at the examples from the listening text in Exercise 4 and answer the questions.

1   *I really don't mind it, **as long as** it isn't for an extended period of time.*

2   *I'd just have to phone someone, **otherwise** I'd go crazy!*

3   *I reckon being alone is never really a bad thing, **provided that** you've got something positive to do.*

4   ***Suppose** I got home after lunch and there was no one there, that'd be OK until about eight o'clock.*

5   ***Imagine** spending a day without seeing anyone, how would you survive?*

6   *I couldn't go to the cinema on my own **unless** it was a film I really wanted to see …*

i   What kind of conditional (first or second) is each of the sentences?

ii   In which of the sentences can you substitute the highlighted expressions with *if*?

iii How would you rewrite the other sentences to include the word *if*?

b) Circle the correct answers.

1   I'll tell you (*provided*) / *unless* / *supposing* you don't tell anyone.

2   *Suppose / Otherwise / Unless* you could be an animal. What animal would you be?

3   I won't speak to you *unless / otherwise / as long as* you apologise.

4   Go to the doctor, *imagine / otherwise / provided* it could get nasty.

5   *As long as / Imagine / Otherwise* you didn't have school today. What would you do?

6   You'll be fine *unless / otherwise / as long as* you do what I tell you.

c) Rewrite the sentences so that they include the words in the brackets. Change the words and the word order so that the meaning is the same.

1   I'll go to the cinema with you if you promise to help me with my homework afterwards. (provided)

   I'll go to the cinema with you provided that you promise to help me with my homework afterwards.

2   If I don't get some time to myself I'll never finish this book. (otherwise)

3   I don't mind being alone if I've got a good book to read. (as long as)

4   What would you do if you got abandoned on a desert island? (suppose)

5   If you had a week of holidays now, what would you do? (imagine)

6   I would never go on holiday alone if I didn't have to. (unless)

d) Rewrite sentences 1, 2 and 3 from Exercise 6c using *unless*.

e) Now rewrite sentences 1 and 2 from Exercise 6c using *as long as*.

7 Speak

a) Write the number of the activities 1–8 in the grid. Do you prefer to do them alone or with someone else?

1   listening to music
2   reading
3   going to a rock concert
4   studying
5   doing exercise
6   watching TV
7   going on holiday
8   making plans

Best done alone	←									→	Best done with others

b) Compare your grid with your partner. Take it in turns to talk about your reasons. Award yourself a point each time you use a conditional sentence. Who can get the most points?

'I don't mind watching TV with my mum as long as she doesn't keep asking me silly questions about the programme.'

8 Song

(a) Look at the man in the picture and answer the questions.

1 Who do you think this man is and how did he get here?
2 How do you think he survives from day to day?
3 What do you think the future holds for him?

(b) You are going to hear a song called *Message in a Bottle*. Look at the picture in Exercise 8a and decide how the words in the box are connected to the theme of the song. Use a dictionary if you need to.

> note   shore   alone   rescue   SOS   hope   washed up   loneliness
> castaway   island   lonely   home   castaways

(c) 🔊 Listen to the song and complete the sentences with the words from Exercise 8b. You will use some words more than once. Then listen again and check.

Message in a Bottle by The Police

Did you know ...?

From the late 1970s to the mid 1980s The Police were one of the biggest bands in the UK, if not the whole world. Songs like *Don't Stand So Close To Me*, *Roxanne*, *Every Little Thing She Does is Magic* and *Every Breath You Take* made the band a household name in many countries. *Message In A Bottle* is perhaps the most famous song from their second album *Regatta De Blanc*. Although The Police played their last official show in 1985, their lead singer Gordon Sumner (more commonly known as Sting) has gone on to enjoy a highly successful solo career and is one of the world's most respected musicians.

Just a ¹ _____ lost at sea oh
An ² _____ day
Another ³ _____ day
No one here but me oh
More ⁴ _____
Than any man could bear
⁵ _____ me before I
Fall into despair

[Chorus:]
I'll send an ⁶ _____ to the world
I'll send an ⁷ _____ to the world
I hope that someone gets my
I hope that someone gets my
I hope that someone gets my
Message in a bottle yeah
Message in a bottle yeah

A year has passed
Since I wrote my ⁸ _____
I should have known it
Right from the start
Only ⁹ _____
Can keep me together
Love can mend your life but
Love can break your heart

[Repeat chorus]

Woke up this morning
Don't believe what I saw
A hundred million bottles
¹⁰ _____ upon my ¹¹ _____ oh
Seems I'm not ¹² _____
In being ¹³ _____
A hundred million ¹⁴ _____
Looking for a ¹⁵ _____

[Repeat chorus]

(d) Work with a partner. What do you think this song is a metaphor for? Use the lyrics to help you invent a story explaining who this person is and why they feel this way. What was the SOS they sent out? How does the story end?

9 Write

a Work with a partner. Read the leaflet and discuss what it is for. What techniques are used to attract the readers' interests?

Make Time to Make Friends

Gap Year – Open Day (Saturday 12 July)
Develop yourself through sharing with others

* Want to take a break from studying? Looking for the experience of a lifetime?
* Then a gap year might just well be the thing for you. It was for these students.

'I have just returned from the most amazing, eye-opening five months of my life! The Dominican Republic is a beautiful country with some of the most friendly people I have ever met.'
Ash Thompson, Bristol

'Why can't life be just one gap year after another?'
Holly Grainger, Southampton

If you, ... like thousands of other students, feel the time has come to reward yourself with a fascinating trip abroad which gives you a great opportunity to learn another language, meet exciting people from many countries, and spend your time perhaps more meaningfully than ever, come to this **Gap Year Open Day**.

Join us and find out more!

* Join our video conferencing. We'll connect you directly with our project leaders in 12 different countries.
* Talk to students who have just come back from their gap years. Let them take you around the globe with their stories and photos.
* Take part in our Q and A session. It's your chance to ask the questions you want answering.
* Pick up a brochure detailing all the projects we run and how to apply for one of them.

Interested? We're sure you are. See you soon.

b Read the leaflet again. Which of the following are you likely to find in a well written leaflet? Write ✓ (yes) or ✗ (no) in the boxes.

1 very formal language ☐
2 abbreviations ☐
3 rhetorical questions ☐
4 formal language ☐
5 catchy slogans ☐

6 encouragement to do something ☐
7 the writer's address and the date of writing ☐
8 titles, subtitles, bullet pointing ☐
9 lots of adjectives ☐
10 imperatives ☐

c You are managing a summer project for school children during the long summer holidays. The project includes sport and recreational activities. This is the third year you've been doing this and you've already had plenty of happy customers.

Write a leaflet to explain what the project is about and also to motivate students to find out more.

Use the model in Exercise 9a to help you. Write 200–250 words.

Module 3 Check your progress

1 Grammar

(a) Put the words in the correct order to make sentences.

1 finest / the / generation / his / he's / actor / of / undoubtedly
He's undoubtedly the finest actor of his generation.

2 wallet / to / appear / I / lost / have / my

3 to / a / decision / with / seems / he / be / disappointed / bit / my

4 a / decision / was / unquestionably / it / terrible

5 is / for / this / century / discovery / most / undoubtedly / the / important / a

6 happy / be / very / something / appear / to / about / they

7 we / have / it / no / chance / of / more / seems / winning / any

8 the / has / been / life / unquestionably / my / best / this / day / of

[ ] [7]

(b) Cross out any wrong options and tick sentences where both options are correct.

1 When I was younger I *could / was able to* read for hours. These days I fall asleep after ten minutes. ✓

2 We were tired but we *could / managed to* finish the race. ......

3 He was too far away and we *couldn't / weren't able to* hear anything he was saying. ......

4 We looked for half an hour but eventually we *could / were able to* find a parking space. ......

5 The film was in Arabic and I *wasn't able / didn't manage to* understand anything. ......

6 We had a school uniform but on Fridays we *could / managed to* wear anything. ......

7 Sorry I *couldn't / wasn't able to* come to your party but I was busy. ......

8 The questions were easy but I panicked. I *couldn't / wasn't able to* remember anything. ......

[ ] [7]

(c) Rewrite the sentences using the beginning given.

1 I had just sat down with a cup of tea when the telephone rang.
No sooner

2 Please don't tell him where I am under any circumstances.
Under no circumstances ....

3 I've never heard such rubbish.
Never ....

4 He was late to my party and he forgot to bring any music too.
Not only ....

5 I rarely get up before midday on a Sunday.
Rarely ....

6 We were not allowed to go into the woods on any account.
On no account ....

7 We won't only get free tickets, we'll get to meet the band too.
Not only ....

8 They had just arrived home when the police car arrived.
No sooner ....

[ ] [7]

(d) Use the two sentences to write a mixed conditional sentence.

1 We lost the match. We're not the champions.
If we hadn't lost the match, we'd be the champions.

2 He knows first aid. He saved my life.

3 I speak Spanish. I understood the film.

4 I missed the plane. I'm not in Hawaii now.

5 She's a vegetarian. She wasn't able to eat anything.

6 I like children. I enjoyed the party.

7 I forgot to take an aspirin. I've got a terrible headache.

8 I didn't go to bed until 2am. I'm really tired today.

[ ] [7]

(e) Rewrite the sentences using the words in brackets.

1 What would you ask the Prime Minister if you could ask her one question? (imagine)
Imagine if you could ask the Prime Minister one question, what would you ask her?

2 I'll tell you everything if you promise not to say who told you. (provided)

3 What would you do if it happened to you? (suppose)

4 If she doesn't take this antidote, she'll die before we get to the hospital. (otherwise)

5 Only use this if you really have to. (unless)

6 We have to leave now. Otherwise we'll miss the train. (if)

7 I'll go to the party with you if you promise to give me a lift home. (as long as)

8 Unless he apologises, I'll never speak to him again. (if)

[ ] [7]

2 Vocabulary

a Complete the crossword and find the mystery word.

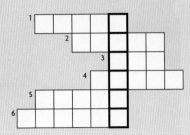

1 You can tell when my baby brother is tired because he _____
2 Careful! That dog _____
3 Don't _____ your eyes. You'll make them sore.
4 You should see a doctor. That's a nasty _____ you've got there.
5 He's so fast. _____ and you'll miss him.
6 I wish you wouldn't _____ with your hair when I'm speaking to you.
7 The mystery word is _____

| 7 |

b Read each sentence and mark the following sentence (*T*) true or (*F*) false.

1 It looks like our holiday plans are going to fall through this year.
There's a good chance we'll go on holiday. _F_
2 He had problems learning to read and write and he overcame them.
He still can't read or write. _____
3 It looked like I had no chance of winning. Somehow I pulled it off.
I won the race. _____
4 I went for an interview for the job and I blew it.
I got the job. _____
5 I thought I'd mess up my driving test but I didn't.
I thought I'd fail my driving test. _____
6 The course didn't fulfil my expectations.
I was disappointed by the course. _____
7 He was in a band for ten years. They never really made it to the top.
His band was really successful for a while. _____
8 Every time I open my computer something goes wrong.
I'm not very good with computers. _____

| 7 |

c Use the words in the box in the correct form to complete the sentences.

> slouch ~~pant~~ puny strength short-sighted
> speed of light squint vision breath

1 You just have to put on your walking shoes and the dog starts _panting_ .
2 He's so strong I sometimes think he's got superhuman _____ .
3 I think you need glasses. You're starting to _____ when you read.
4 I wish I hadn't run. I'm really short of _____ now.
5 If you don't stop _____ when you sit, you'll have back problems when you're older.
6 You're really _____ . You need to go to the gym and get some muscles on you.
7 How am I supposed to know what the letter says? It's in an envelope and I haven't got X-ray _____ .
8 I can't read what that sign says. I'm _____ .
9 I asked for some help with the washing up and he was out of the kitchen at the _____ .

| 8 |

d (Circle) the correct option.

1 I've got three months until university starts. How am I going to *empty /* (*fill*) */ make* my time?
2 I really need a break mid-morning. It *makes / gives / gets* me time to think about the rest of the day.
3 He's just *killing / murdering / assassinating* time until *Dr Who* starts.
4 Parents must accompany their children *at / in / on* all times.
5 Just stay calm. I'll be with you in *neither / no / not* time.
6 If you've got some time on your *arms / hands / shoulders*, you could give me some help.
7 Your time's *in / out / up*. You'll have to pay another £1 if you want to go on playing.

| 6 |

How did you do?

Tick (✓) a box for each section.

Total score:	☺	😐	☹
63	Very good	OK	Not very good
Grammar	27 – 35	18 – 26	less than 18
Vocabulary	21 – 28	15– 20	less than 15

Module 4
Youth and old age

YOU WILL LEARN ABOUT ...

- The generation gap between parents and children ....
- The world of cosmetic surgery ....
- How old we will live to be in the future ....
- The Bata Shoe Museum ....
- A trip to the opera ....
- Bagpuss, a famous old TV character ....

✱ Can you match each picture with a topic?

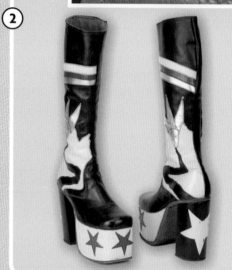

YOU WILL LEARN HOW TO ...

Speak
- Discuss whether each generation thinks differently
- Talk about life choices
- Discuss the advantages and disadvantages of cosmetic surgery
- Talk about a visit to a museum or an art gallery
- Discuss which objects you would choose for a People's Museum for your country
- Take part in a discussion to plan a school trip.
- Brainstorm ideas for an experiment on 'swapping places' among members of a family

Write
- A formal letter to a magazine
- A report and an article
- Notes for different situations
- A cinquain or a meaningless proverb

Read
- A magazine article about the differences between the younger and older generations
- A magazine article giving people's opinions about cosmetic surgery
- A newspaper text about ageing today and in the future
- An article describing a father and son's feelings during a pop concert and an opera performance

Listen
- Interviews with people giving their opinions about the Age Wars
- An expert talking about ageing in the future
- Three members of a band discussing the cover of their new album
- A radio programme titled *Our Heritage*

Use grammar

Can you match the names of the grammar points with the examples?

Future perfect

Future continuous

Alternative ways of referring to the future

Past tenses with hypothetical meaning

Substitution

My brother's **off** to Australia next month.

She'll probably be sixty before she'**ll have saved** enough money to buy a house!

Viewers were asked to vote and thousands did **so**.

He certainly **won't be voting** for that man in the coming elections.

It's **time** we learned to accept new technologies.

Use vocabulary

Can you think of two more examples for each topic?

Life choices	Commonly confused words	Old and new	Teenspeak
drop out of school	effect / affect	contemporary	Whatever
take out a loan	sensitive / sensible	old-fashioned	dorky
....	....	....	....
....	....	....	....

13 The age wars

* Future perfect / future continuous review
* Alternative ways of referring to the future
* Vocabulary: life choices

1 Read and listen

(a) Look at the photos and title of the article. What do you think the age wars might be?

(b) 🔊 Read the text and put the paragraphs in order. Listen to check.

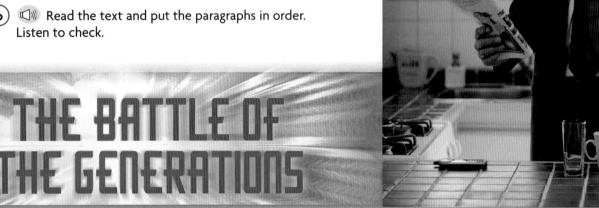

THE BATTLE OF THE GENERATIONS

☐ 58-year-old Gerry enjoys a leisurely Friday morning breakfast as he sips his tea and browses the newspaper for property prices overseas. He's in no hurry to get to work. As a senior partner in the company he joined straight from university nearly 40 years ago, no one's going to mind if he arrives an hour or two late.

☐ Gerry never had to lose sleep over paying for further education. It was all free in his day. Furthermore the house that he bought for around £20,000 back in the 1970s is worth over a million now. These days his only concern is the news that a local politician has put forward a plan to build cheap accommodation in the fields outside the village. He'll certainly not be voting for that fellow in the coming elections. Mind you, he'll have bought a villa in Marbella by the time he retires. Yes, he'll be all right. He'll be living a life of luxury on the beaches of southern Spain when he's 65.

☐ Gerry has no such concerns as he climbs into his big four wheel drive and goes the half a mile down to the local station to catch the train to work. He'll get a taxi the other end too. He's worked hard and won't have some green activist telling him how to lead his life.

☐ Gerry puts on his coat to leave the office. His secretary reminds him that he's seeing Josephine the next day. Josephine, his 18-year-old daughter with all her wonderful ideas on how to save the world. He sighs to himself: when will that girl start taking her future seriously?

☐ Josephine finds herself daydreaming at college about having children. She's in no hurry but she knows she would love to settle down and have children one day. She'd love a big family but will she be able to afford one? Besides, with the overpopulation of the world, maybe it would be better just to have one. On the way home from college she reads an article in the paper about the latest war over oil and starts feeling bad that her child, when it finally comes, will be living in a world that's probably on its last legs.

☐ She checks her diary: oh no, her parents are coming over at the weekend. More lectures from her dad about doing something sensible at university, by which he means something that will get her a good job and make her money. Just because he helps her with the rent, he thinks he has the right to interfere with her life. Welcome to the age wars.

☐ On the bus, Josephine starts worrying about her future. She is starting a course in conservation at university in September. She loves nature and wants to work in that field, but she knows the jobs aren't well-paid. How is she ever going to pay back the university loans? And of course, one day far in the future, she'd like to own a house. She doesn't know much about the property market but she does know that house prices are crazy. She'll probably be 60 before she'll have saved enough money to buy one! She's sure she's too young to have to worry about these things.

☐ 50 miles away from Gerry in his leafy suburban house, Josephine grabs a pot of yogurt as she rushes out of her one-bedroom rented flat in a grotty part of London and runs down the street to catch the bus to college. Not that she'd take the car even if she could afford one. Besides the ridiculous cost of getting into and parking in Central London, she's concerned about global warming and doesn't want her exhaust fumes contributing to the problem.

2 Grammar

Future perfect / future continuous review

a Look at the sentences from the text. Which are examples of the future continuous and which are examples of the future perfect?

1 *He'll **be living** a life of luxury on the beaches of southern Spain when he's 65.*
2 *He'll **have bought** a villa in Majorca by the time he retires.*
3 *She'll probably be 60 before she'll **have saved** enough money to buy a house!*
4 *Her child **will be living** in a world that's on its last legs.*

b Complete the sentences using the verb in brackets in the future continuous or future perfect tense.

1 You can have the newspaper in ten minutes. I *'ll have finished* (finish) it by then.
2 I'll be in Chile this time next year.
   I _____ (finish) university and I _____ (travel) around the world.
3 After my parents have seen this report card I _____ (not go) on holiday with you.
4 She _____ (have) the baby by then and they _____ (try) to get used to life without sleep.
5 We have to meet up this year. Otherwise we _____ (not see) each other for five years.
6 This time next week we _____ (move) and we _____ (live) in our new house.
7 **A:** They _____ (arrive) by now. Shall I give them a call?
   B: No, it's too late. They _____ (sleep).
8 **A:** Do you think you _____ (drive) next month?
   B: No. I _____ (not pass) my test by then.

c Read the short profile of Gerry. Find and correct four factual mistakes.

Gerry's in his early fifties. He has a good life. He's a partner in company he's been working in for nearly thirty years. He lives in a big house in a desirable suburb of London and drives a big car. He is looking forward to his retirement, which he plans to spend living in a villa he wants to buy in Greece.

Gerry feels he's entitled to his lifestyle. He has worked hard all his life and feels he deserves a little luxury. He's not really concerned about problems such as the environment or how young people are supposed to afford houses. In fact, his only real worry in life is his daughter Josephine. He wishes she would start a family soon.

d Write a short profile of Josephine. Use the passage about Gerry as a model.

e Circle the best definition for each of the words from the text.

1 browse (paragraph 1) *read quickly / read at leisure*
2 suburban (paragraph 7) *in the city centre / outside the city centre*
3 grotty (paragraph 7) *elegant / dirty and in bad condition*
4 exhaust fumes (paragraph 7) *the smoke that comes out of a car / transport habits*
5 lose sleep over (paragraph 2) *worry about / work hard for*
6 retire (paragraph 2) *stop working / change jobs*
7 daydream (paragraph 5) *sleep during the day / get lost in a world of thoughts*
8 on its last legs (paragraph 5) *in a bad condition / recovering from an illness*

3 Listen

(a) Work with a partner. Can you remember the problems that Gerry and Josephine have from Exercise 1?

(b) 🔊 Listen to six people giving their opinions about the article and tick the correct boxes in the table.

	from Gerry's generation	from Josephine's generation
Speaker one		
Speaker two		
Speaker three		
Speaker four		
Speaker five		
Speaker six		

(c) 🔊 Listen again and mark the statements *T* (true) or *F* (false). Correct the false statements.

Speaker one thinks:

1 The real reason he's going to lose his job is because he's too old. ☐

2 If he sells his house, he'll have enough money for his retirement. ☐

Speaker two thinks:

3 His father gave him some good advice. ☐

4 Young people have to make choices too early in their life. ☐

Speaker three thinks:

5 Older people are responsible for some serious social problems. ☐

6 Tax payers' money should be spent differently. ☐

Speaker four thinks:

7 Josephine has nothing to worry about. ☐

8 Nuclear weapons are a more serious danger than global warming. ☐

Speaker five thinks:

9 The older generation are to blame for ruining the planet. ☐

10 Any inheritance that she gets will come too late in life for her. ☐

Speaker six thinks:

11 His brother is crazy to want to buy a house. ☐

12 He might go and live abroad when he finishes school. ☐

4 Grammar

Alternative ways of referring to the future

1 *I'm 55 and I'm about to lose my job very soon.*

2 *My brother's off to Australia next month.*

3 *They say that house prices are due to fall.*

4 *If people keep on describing this situation as a war, things are bound to get worse.*

5 *I am supposed to inherit the family house when my parents pass on.*

6 *I'm thinking of changing courses.*

(a) Look at the examples in Exercise 4 from the listening. All these sentences refer to the future. Which sentence talks about:

a a future expectation: things that are generally expected to happen sometime in the future (x2)

b future travel plans

c a prediction of a certain future (as the speaker sees it)

d the very immediate future

e a possible future event that is being considered in the present.

There are several other ways of referring to the future besides *will* and *going to*. Expressions such as *about to, off to, due to, bound to, supposed to* and *thinking of* used with the verb *to be* all can be used to refer to different types of future.

Of course, if we use these expressions with *was* and *were* then we create other possible ways of talking about the future in the past. (see Unit 2)

I was supposed to arrive at ten but the train was late.

They were off on holiday so they didn't have time to chat.

You could tell from the way they were playing that they were bound to win.

b Circle the correct answers.

1 We're *off to* / *bound to* / *thinking of* Spain on holiday tomorrow. I can't wait.

2 Their plane's *about to* / *due to* / *off to* land at two but it's been delayed.

3 I was *about to* / *thinking of* / *supposed to* changing my career but I've decided against it.

4 Tomorrow's a holiday so it's *due to* / *about to* / *bound to* rain.

5 We were *supposed to* / *off to* / *thinking of* be going out tonight but Jane's not feeling too well.

6 Susie looks so sad, as if she's *off to* / *about to* / *thinking of* start crying.

7 I'm *bound to* / *supposed to* / *about to* give him an answer tomorrow but I still haven't decided.

8 I was *about to* / *off to* / *bound to* leave when he phoned.

5 Vocabulary

Life choices

a Match the verbs 1–8 with the words a–h to make meaningful expressions. There may be more than one possibility.

1 settle   a careers
2 take out   b a year off
3 pay off   c student loans
4 take   d early retirement
5 start   e a family
6 change   f school
7 drop out of   g college/university
8 leave   h down

b Use expressions from Exercise 5a to complete the texts. You may have to change the verb form.

> I finish school next year and then the real decisions start, I suppose. I want to go to university but I want to ¹ *take a year off* and see the world first. My dad thinks it's a terrible idea but then he would, because he started work as soon as he was able to. My mum just wants me to find a nice man, get married and ² _____ as soon as possible. She also wants me to ³ _____ soon because she wants grandchildren. She'll just have to wait on that one.

> I think the person I most admire in our family is my uncle. He ⁴ _____ at an early age and didn't even go to university. He's also ⁵ _____ about three times – he's a teacher at the moment but is already talking about doing something different. He's also really smart too. He's been saving money since he was 16 so he'll be able to ⁶ _____ – probably when he's about 55. I'm sure this is something he really wants to do.

6 Speak

a Work with a partner. Who do you think is asking each question? Who are they asking and why?

1 'So what age do you plan to retire then? What on earth will you do with all that free time?'

2 'Do you think you will have your own house or flat one day?'

3 'Would you like to change careers sometime in your life? What would your new job be?'

b Imagine what your grandmother or grandfather were like when they were the age you are now. How do you think their answers would be different?

Literature in mind

7 Read

(a) Read the two poems and decide whether the writer is positive or negative about growing old in each one.

(a) *Beautiful Old Age*
D. H. Lawrence (1885–1930)

It ought to be lovely to be old
to be full of the peace that comes of experience
and wrinkled ripe fulfilment.
The wrinkled smile of completeness that follows a life
lived undaunted and unsoured with accepted lies.
They would ripen like apples, and be scented like
pippins* in their old age.
Soothing, old people should be, like apples
when one is tired of love.
Fragrant like yellowing leaves, and dim with the soft
stillness and satisfaction of autumn.
And a girl should say:
It must be wonderful to live and grow old.
Look at my mother, how rich and still she is! —
And a young man should think: By Jove
my father has faced all weathers, but it's been a life!

(*pippin = a kind of apple)

(b) *A Madrigal*
William Shakespeare (1546–1616)

Crabbed Age and Youth
Cannot live together:
Youth is full of pleasance,
Age is full of care;
Youth like summer morn,
Age like winter weather,
Youth like summer brave,
Age like winter bare;
Youth is full of sport,
Age's breath is short,
Youth is nimble, Age is lame;
Youth is hot and bold,
Age is weak and cold,
Youth is wild, and Age is tame:
Age, I do abhor thee;
Youth, I do adore thee:
O! my Love, my Love is young!
Age, I do defy thee!
O sweet shepherd, hie thee,
For methinks thou stay'st too long.

(b) Read *Beautiful Old Age* again and find words with these meanings.

1 with lines on the face
2 not frightened
3 making something less painful
4 smelling nice
5 not giving much light

(c) The poem makes a strong link between people and nature. Find parts of the poem where this link is made, and say why you think the poet does this.

(d) Read *A Madrigal* again. There are some words that are rare in modern English. Match the words with their meaning.

1	crabbed	a	I think
2	pleasance	b	you (subject)
3	morn	c	bad-tempered
4	abhor	d	go quickly
5	thee	e	hate
6	hie	f	morning
7	methinks	g	enjoyment
8	thou	h	you (object)

(e) The poem talks about youth and age as if they were actual people. Find parts of the poem where this happens, and say why you think the poet does this.

(f) Work with a partner. Discuss your answers to these questions.

1 Which poem do you prefer, and why?
2 Were either of the poems written by someone who was old, do you think? Why do you think so?
3 Would you want to read another poem by either of the two poets? Why / Why not?

8 Write

A reader wrote a response to the editor of the magazine which published the article *The Battle of the Generations* in Exercise 1.

a Read the letter and answer the questions.

1 Is the person who wrote the letter a younger or older person?
2 How does the writer suggest the problem of housing costs could be dealt with?
3 What does the writer say about how governments spend money raised through taxes?
4 What does the writer consider to be the biggest problem that everyone is facing?

Dear Sir,

I was intrigued by your article entitled *The Battle of the Generations* and feel I would like to reply to some of the ideas put forward in it. As a student in my early 20s, I was happy to see that someone is taking the problems my generation are facing seriously, although I disagree that all elderly people are as smug and selfish as the (fictional?) Gerry in the article.

One of the things that was mentioned is the question of housing. It is clear that prices in this country are excessively high and that first time buyers (as I hope to soon be) will have great difficulty in entering the market. The obvious solution, or part of it at least, would be to increase taxation on second homes to a point that makes it simply prohibitive. However this would make the government unpopular, and therefore no government is likely ever to take the risk. This is a great shame, in my view.

A further point that the article raises is that of students needing to provide their own funding for university education. As I am currently struggling to save some money for university, I have to say that this makes little sense: people are denied the benefits of higher education (benefits not only for themselves but also for the country in general) when we continue to spend enormous amounts of money on the military. A return to the basic system of providing education for anyone who wants it can only be a good thing.

Finally, it is suggested that older sections of society do not show concern for environmental issues. My own experience – looking around me and talking to people of various ages, my parents and my friend's parents included – indicates that there is absolutely no relationship between attitudes to the environment and the age of the person concerned. It is specifically the environment which I believe illustrates most clearly the need for people of all ages to put aside their differences – whether sex, colour, race or religion – and work together for the benefit of everyone here now, and of future generations. Otherwise there may well be no future generations.

Yours faithfully,
Althea Graves

---

b Look at the first sentence of the letter again.

I was intrigued by your article entitled The Battle of the Generations *and feel I would like to reply to some of the ideas put forward in it.*

<u>Underline</u> the following grammar points in the sentence.

1 the passive voice
2 a past participle used as an adjective after a noun

c Read the letter again and find more examples of the parts of speech mentioned in Exercise 8b.

d Here are three very short letters in a magazine. Choose one of them and write a reply to the editor of the magazine, agreeing or disagreeing with the opinion stated. Write 200–250 words.

Dear Sir,
People who live in cities should not be allowed to have dogs.
Yours faithfully,
Ivor Cox

Dear Sir,
No more money should be spent on guns or the army.
Yours faithfully,
James Mason

Dear Sir,
I believe the age for driving should be raised to 21.
Yours faithfully,
Mrs A Jones

For your portfolio

14 The beauty hunters

* Past tenses with hypothetical meaning
* Vocabulary: commonly confused words

1 Read and listen

(a) Work with a partner. Make a list of the advantages and disadvantages of cosmetic surgery.

(b) Read the texts and match the titles with the paragraphs. There is one title you do not need to use.

A They should be ashamed ☐

B There are two sides to all stories ☐

C She looks so grotesque ☐

D A new start ☐

E What's wrong with it? ☐

F Don't be fooled by 'perfection' ☐

Hard talk – cosmetic surgery

This week we look at a phenomenal trend hitting our nation – more and more people are spending a fortune on cosmetic surgery. Read for yourself what our readers think.

1 Dr Ken Berrick, Aesthetic surgeon

I've treated thousands of patients at my clinic and they all wanted the same thing. They wanted to look better, and become more confident, to be more assertive and get ahead in their careers. They wanted more friends. In short, they wanted to lead happier lives. They all knew that cosmetic surgery could help them achieve this, which is why they came to us and, of course, we advise our patients carefully. And I can say with great satisfaction that the overwhelming majority of our patients are more than happy with the results of their surgery. The service we have given them has not only changed their looks, but significantly raised their self-esteem and transformed their lives. Of course there are people who criticise the use of cosmetic surgery. But I fail to see what's wrong with using medical science to enhance our human capacities and characteristics. It's time we learned to accept new technologies and how they can help us.

2 Dr Elisabeth McKenna, Psychologist

Cosmetic surgery is not something to be entered into lightly. Unfortunately, in this modern world, we have become obsessed with very narrow standards of beauty. We are bombarded daily with images of celebrities who have immaculate faces and stunning bodies and who never seem to age. We forget the fact that most of these images are the result of sophisticated photo manipulation, driven by the incredibly powerful beauty industry. We are all different – why should we all look the same? Isn't there more to life than undergoing surgery in order to have the same boring face that everybody else wants to have? If only we could celebrate diversity, instead of sameness. Then we'd all end up feeling better about ourselves.

3 Debbie Caron, Student

Yes, it's fake! That's what I told my friends when they started asking me about my nose job. I'd always been sensitive about my nose, but it took me a long time before I decided to go for cosmetic surgery. I took advice from several doctors and after careful consultation I finally decided to have it done. I had been saving money from my part time job and my parents helped me out with the rest. It was quite

c ◁)) Read the text again. Who mentions the following? There may be more than one person for each answer. Listen to check.

1 Cosmetic surgery can often go wrong.
2 Cosmetic surgery can have really positive effects on people's lives.
3 It can be difficult to stop having cosmetic surgery once you start.
4 There are more important uses for medical science.
5 We're all trying to look the same.
6 It's silly to try and stop progress.
7 We're all the victims of marketing campaigns.
8 The whole industry is really just about money.

d Match the words 1–8 from the text with the definitions a–h.

1 enhance
2 immaculate
3 vanity
4 overwhelming
5 fake
6 consultation
7 wrinkles
8 unscrupulous

a perfect, without any mistakes
b when you discuss something with someone to get their advice or opinion
c small lines in the skin caused by old age
d to improve the quality, amount or strength of something
e behaving in a way that is dishonest or unfair in order to get what you want
f very great or very large
g not real, but made to look real
h the act of giving great importance to the way you look

Discussion box

Work in pairs or small groups. Discuss these questions together.

1 Do you agree that surgery should be carried out for medical purposes only? Why / Why not?
2 Do you agree we should 'celebrate diversity, not sameness'? Give reasons for your opinions.
3 Which famous people do you admire who do not look stunning and immaculate?

expensive but I don't regret a penny of it. My level of self-confidence has risen enormously. In fact, I wish I'd had it done a few years ago. I'm sure I wouldn't have been teased so much at school. Now I can start university next year with a new look, though of course, it's the same old me underneath.

4 Sue Kennedy, Student

A friend of mine's mum had a facelift a few years ago and at the time, I have to admit, she looked a lot better. She had quite a lot of wrinkles for her age and the surgery definitely made her look younger. In fact, I even joked with my mum about her doing the same thing. But then my friend's mum started having silicone injections every month in her cheeks to make her cheekbones look higher. These injections affect people in different ways. Immediately following the injections, her face would swell, but the silicone would always go down the next day and she still looked OK. However, over time the shape of her face started changing and it didn't look

good. She started to look like someone who'd had bad cosmetic surgery. We all wish she would stop but she still does it, even though she looks awful. I think the problem is that she's addicted and can't see what it's doing to her. I'm glad my mum didn't take my advice.

5 Danny Glass, Student

It makes me really angry to think of the millions of people who spend a fortune on what some people wrongly call 'body sculpting'. It's surgery, and surgery should be carried out for medical purposes, not vanity. I would rather all the money spent on cosmetic surgery was available to treat people around the world who are in need but can't get proper medical treatment. Furthermore, there are thousands of unscrupulous and under-qualified practitioners out there who only care about getting as rich as possible as quickly as possible. They don't care about the psychological and physical damage they do. The whole industry makes me sick. We should do the sensible thing and ban it.

2 Grammar

Past tenses with hypothetical meaning

(a) Look at these sentences from the text and then answer the questions.

a If only we could celebrate diversity, instead of sameness.

b We all wish she would stop.

c I'd rather all the money spent on cosmetic surgery was available to treat people around the world.

d It took me a long time before I decided to go for cosmetic surgery.

e It's time we learned to accept new technologies and how they can help us.

1 Which one refers to a past event?

2 What time do the others refer to?

(b) The past tense can be used with different expressions to talk about hypothetical present situations. These expressions include: *wish, if only, it's time* and *would rather/sooner*.

Complete the rule with words from the box.

| desire   annoyance   change   emphasise   preference |

Rule:

- *Wish / If only* + past tense are used to express a .... or regret about a present action or situation.
  If only my nose wasn't so big.
  They are used with *could* to talk about (lack of) ability/permission.
  He wishes he could afford a nose job.
- They are often used with *would* to express .... at the situation.
  I wish you wouldn't talk to me like that.
- *It's time + subject + past tense* is used to suggest that someone should take action to .... a present situation.
  It's time you stopped worrying about your looks and got on with life.
  It's time can be used with other patterns:
  It's time to stop worrying about your looks and get on with life. (infinitive + present)
  It's time for you to stop worrying about your looks ... (for + subject + infinitive)
- We can .... this expression by using *about* or *high*.
  It's high/about time you stopped worrying about your looks and got on with life.
- *Would rather/sooner + subject + past simple* is used to express a .... for a hypothetical situation or event over a real one.
  I'd rather/sooner she spent the money for her nose job on a holiday in Indonesia for all of us.

(c) Rewrite the sentences using the word (or words) in brackets.

1 Your jacket is really old. (It's time)
  It's time you bought a new jacket.

2 Don't interrupt while I'm speaking. (I'd rather)

3 Why don't you ever listen to what I say! (wish)

4 We don't even know his name. (If only)

5 Come on. We've got to make a decision. (It's time)

6 I never seem to have enough time. (wish)

7 Please don't drive so fast. (I'd rather)

8 Why can't I make her understand? (If only)

(d) Work with a partner. Look at the example conversation.

A: *I've been studying so hard recently that I haven't even been able to go to the cinema.*

B: *It's time you put down your books and had some fun.*

A: *I know, but I've got a big exam next week.*

B: *OK, but if you don't relax, ...*

Student A: Read one of the statements from the list below to Student B.

Student B: Reply using one of the expressions from Exercise 2b.

1 My best friend keeps complaining that I never have time for him/her.

2 None of my friends seems to be available when I phone them, but they expect me to help them whenever they want.

3 There is a problem with my computer – I have lost lots of files recently.

4 My parents don't allow me to use the phone after 8pm in the evening.

5 My brother constantly takes things from my room without asking.

Swap roles when you have completed all five conversations.

3 Listen and speak

(a) Look at the photographs. How old do you think the people in the photos are? How old do you think people will live to in the future?

(b) 🔊 What do you think biogerentology is? Listen to an expert and check your ideas. What for you are the most surprising things he says?

(c) 🔊 Listen again and (circle) the correct answers a, b or c.

1 The key question for biogerentology is how lives in the future can be made longer:
   a for as many people as possible and for as long as possible
   b for people who are healthy and lead a healthy life
   c for those people who have the financial means to pay for special treatments

2 One of the crucial questions concerning life extension is whether:
   a humans will have the ability to live up to the age of 150
   b the creating of life prolonging methods will be banned or not
   c there will be a dramatic battle over life and death in the coming century

3 According to the expert people will become significantly older,
   a stay healthy and fit, but their memory will not be very acute
   b stay healthy and fit, and will have very acute memory
   c and have acute memory, but will be a lot less healthy and fit than younger people

4 People will eat:
   a a diet that is not very tasty, but very healthy
   b a diet of pills and other chemicals only
   c delicious foods that contain nutrients and medication

5 Scientists recently managed to stop the production of cholesterol in monkeys and this:
   a gives hope that one day the cases of heart disease will be considerably reduced
   b offers people a lot more choices through biochemical pharmaceuticals
   c proves that genetic diseases such as Alzheimer's will be a thing of the past

(d) Work with a partner and discuss the questions.

1 What is the moral argument in the listening in Exercise 3? Which side do you agree with?

2 If you could have a conversation with your great-great-grandparents, what would you ask them about?

3 What advantages or disadvantages would you see in a world as described in the interview? Give your reasons.

4 Vocabulary
Commonly confused words

(a) Read these sentences from the text on page 96 and (circle) the correct word. Check your answers in the text.

1 Cosmetic surgery can have really positive *affects* / *effects* on people's lives

2 These injections *effect* / *affect* people in different ways.

3 I'd always been *sensible* / *sensitive* about my nose.

4 We should do the *sensible* / *sensitive* thing and ban it.

5 We *advise* / *advice* our patients carefully.

6 I took *advise* / *advice* from several doctors.

7 Our service has significantly *raised* / *risen* their self-esteem.

8 My level of self-confidence has *raised* / *risen* enormously.

(b) Complete each sentence with a word from the box.

> ensure   lose   lay   insure   prosecute
> ~~loose~~   lie   persecuted

1 The skin on her face was getting _loose_ .

2 Get a nose job – what have you got to .... ?

3 I'm really tired. I'm going to .... down for half an hour.

4 My chickens don't .... many eggs.

5 If you have very valuable things in your house, you should .... them.

6 Save your work regularly to .... that you don't lose anything.

7 Ever since the news broke about the corruption in his company, he has been .... by the media.

8 We .... all shoplifters.

(c) Discuss with your class and teacher any other pairs of words that can be confusing.

Speaking

5 Speak and listen

(a) A band called Liverpool Hotel has recorded a CD called *Rainbow's End*. Here are three possible covers for the CD. Describe each one. Which one do you like best?

(b) 🔊 Listen to the three members of the band discussing the covers. Which one do they choose?

(c) 🔊 Listen again and complete the sentences with the phrases in the box.

> exactly   I mean   I'd have thought   though
> we're going round in circles   tell you what
> the thing is   to tell you the truth
> on the other hand   to be honest

1 .... let's just kind of spread them out – like ... this ... and then we can ... I mean.

2 I thought it was quite nice – .... , it's not my favourite but it's not too bad.

3 True. But .... is it so important to have a picture that's got something to do with the band name?

4 .... , we've got to choose the one that really says something about us as a band, don't you reckon?

5 OK, well, ... , I don't think any of these say much about us.

6 Well, ... , no, I don't think it is entirely.

7 I think .... a bit here, aren't we?

8 GIRL: True. But on the other hand, is it so important to have a picture that's got something to do with the band name?
BOY: .... it was vital. It's our first CD, after all, so we need to ...

9 GIRL: This one? It's a bit gloomy isn't it? Look at it, brown and grey and dark ...
BOY: .... – just like our songs! That's what's so good about it!

10 GIRL: OK. Wow, they're all right, aren't they?
BOY: Not bad, I really don't like this one, ...

(d) Which phrases are used:

1 to make a suggestion   *tell you what ...*
2 to introduce a contrasting idea
3 to try to get the conversation back to the main topic
4 to give an opinion
5 to add the idea of contrast after stating a fact or opinion
6 to introduce and soften a negative fact or opinion
7 to agree with what someone has said

(e) Work in a small group. Imagine that you are starting up a new school magazine. Choose a picture for the front cover. Use the phrases from Exercise 5c when appropriate.

(f) Work in a small group. Imagine that you are organising a lottery at your school to raise money for charity. Choose one of these things as first prize.

- free cinema tickets for two people for three months
- free daily meals at a fast food restaurant for two people for three months
- free travel on buses in your town for two people for a month

6 Pronunciation

Stress and intonation

🔊 Turn to page 122.

7 Write

a Work with a partner and discuss the differences between a report and an article. Read the descriptions of reports and articles in 1–8 and write the numbers in the table.

1 a piece of writing on a particular subject in a newspaper or magazine

2 to inform, interest and/or entertain the readers

3 entertaining, containing lots of adjectives, direct quotes if possible, and also narrative bits

4 to inform about a situation or event, often in order to judge the quality of it, and to draw conclusions from it

5 clear and precise title specifying what it is about, sub-titles, date of writing, indication who wrote it

6 columns as in a magazine, catchy headline, could contain visuals

7 a written statement containing a precise description of a situation or an event

8 neutral or formal, must be clear and unambiguous in its message

	report	article
What is it?		
What is its main purpose?		
What is its layout / visual appearance?		
What is its style?		

b You attended a meeting with some of your classmates to discuss a project your class had done on the topic *Art in London*. Read the following notes you made in the meeting and then choose one of the tasks below.

- Visits to museums/galleries: 3 groups – Tate Gallery, Tate Modern and the British Museum, positive feedback, especially from Tate Modern group.

- Internet research: did not go as well as hoped, computer lab not always accessible, problems with other groups wanting to use lab at the same time, talk to principal about this?

- Communication among students: good in principle, towards the end of the project time pressure felt, next time special meetings where problems can be discussed?

- Website for publication of project outcomes: deadline too tight, all the groups behind their schedule, set more realistic new deadline?

- General: great for students and teachers to cooperate outside of normal lessons, good opportunity to get to know each other better!

1 A report for the school principal outlining the good and the bad features of the project and recommending whether any changes should be made if a similar project were to be done again in the future. (200–250 words)

2 An article for the school magazine to give other students at your school the opportunity to learn about the project and also read your personal opinion on the project. (200–250 words)

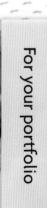

For your portfolio

15 Days gone by

* Substitution: *the ones / so*
* Ellipsis: leaving words out
* Vocabulary: old and new

1 Read and listen

a Look at the items in the photos. Decide what type of museum each of these objects might be found in and why it would be there.

The toy cat might have been the favourite toy of the Queen when she was a child. Maybe it's in a museum about the Royal Family.

①  ②

③  ④  ⑤  ⑥

POEMS: WRITTEN BY WIL. SHAKESPEARE, Gent.

VOTES FOR WOMEN

b 🔊 Read the text and match pictures 1–6 in Exercise 1a with paragraphs A–H. Listen to check.

The People's Museum

[A] *Far too many people view museums as grey and gloomy palaces of the past, full of objects that no one has any real interest in any more, whereas in fact they are places where we can contrast the artefacts of the past with those we see and use today. Of the hundreds of museums in the country, each has its own hidden treasures. Unfortunately all too often these remain unappreciated, gathering dust, unnoticed by the wider public. That was, until now.*

[B] A unique television experiment, the People's Museum has gathered together many of these historic gems and given them new and everlasting life in the virtual world that is the Internet. Led by Paul Martin, a team of reporters uncovered hundreds of extraordinary items representing fascinating local and national history, as well as unique personal stories. Each week, they presented the ones that they felt were worthy of a place in the virtual online museum. Viewers were asked to vote for their favourites, and each week thousands did so. The result was a democratically chosen interactive museum with worldwide access for anyone at any time of the day. Furthermore – no admission charges.

[C] Almost 300 items were selected from more than seventy museums. Although big name museums were visited, such as the Science Museum and the Imperial War Museum, the majority of artefacts were chosen from small, regional museums, since these are the ones where much of the UK's regional identity can be found.

[D] Many of the nominations were objects with an undeniable place in our history. For example, the first ever lifeboat, from Redcar museum, is a reminder of a service that has saved countless lives at sea over the decades. Likewise, a medal given to one of the Suffragettes takes us back to a time when women didn't have the vote and had to fight for their rights. Other objects put forward were from a less distant past. The original Bagpuss from the 1970s was suggested by a viewer with an obvious nostalgia for a misspent childhood in front of the television.

[E] Artefacts from the famous also proved popular. As the father of modern psychiatry, it was perhaps no surprise that Sigmund Freud's sofa was proposed: the original shrink's couch. Likewise, perhaps last century's biggest brain was celebrated when one viewer nominated Albert Einstein's blackboard. Who knows, was this where that legendary equation $E=MC^2$ was first ever written down?

[F] Objects of unquestionable quality also won their place in the museum. For example, when it comes to making violins, one name stands head and shoulders above the rest, Stradivarius, and in the museum you'll find an example of his fine craftsmanship. And of course, no British museum would be complete without the work of this country's greatest ever writer, William Shakespeare. A museum in Leeds supplied an edition of his first folio for online reading.

[G] The eventual winner though, was something much more quintessentially British, the Supermarine Spitfire from the Think Tank Museum in Birmingham. This tiny fighting aircraft might not look much compared to today's stealth fighters, but to many it symbolises the spirit that

(c) Find words or phrases in the text which mean the following.

1 a bit dark and depressing (paragraph A)
2 a jewel; something very pleasing (paragraph B)
3 very different or unusual (paragraph B)
4 a great number (paragraph D)
5 a psychiatrist (paragraph E)
6 happening at the end (paragraph F)
7 typically (paragraph F)
8 looking after something (paragraph H)

helped bring WWII to an end. As one of the programme's presenters commented: 'My colleagues did not really expect the plane to win, and frankly neither did I. However, it's clearly a very special item and reflects a part of our history that those who were there have never forgotten, and which arguably should never be forgotten by any of us.'

[H] The success of the programme was a pleasant surprise to all involved and there are rumours of a part two. A representative of the company that produced the series was asked if another one would be made in the future. 'I certainly hope so,' he said. 'It's my own belief that programmes such as the People's Museum perform an invaluable function: that of convincing people of the importance of safeguarding our past in order to understand better who we are and where we are now.'

But will it be enough to convince people to reassess their opinions of real museums? Let's hope so.

2 Grammar

Substitution: *the ones / so*

(a) We often use words to replace, or substitute, other words or ideas. What do the words in **bold** in each sentence refer to?

1 We can contrast the artefacts of the past with **those** we see and use today. _____*artefacts*_____
2 The majority of artefacts were chosen from small regional museums, since these are **the ones** where much of the UK's regional identity can be found. _____
3 They perform an important function: **that of** convincing people. _____
4 Viewers were asked to vote and thousands **did so**. _____
5 We wanted to restore interest. I hope we have succeeded in **doing so**. _____
6 Will there be another series? I certainly hope **so**. _____
7 They didn't expect the plane to win, and **neither did I**. _____
8 He voted for the Spitfire, and **so did I**. _____

(b) Match the sentences in Exercise 2a with the rules a, b, c and d.

a We can use *do / did + so* instead of a verb phrase – this is quite formal. We often use *think so* or *hope so* – again, *so* replaces a verb phrase. _____
b We can use *so / neither, nor* with a meaning like *also*, to avoid repeating an idea. In this case, *so / neither, nor* comes first and is followed by inversion of subject and object. _____
c In more informal English, for example when we speak, we can use *(the) one / (the) ones* instead of the noun. _____
d In formal contexts such as letters or reports, we can use *that / those* instead of a noun. *That* can't be used for people; *those* can be. _____

(c) Rephrase the underlined parts of these sentences. Sometimes there is more than one possibility.

1 The technology they use is very different from the technology used in the past.

   The technology they use is very different from that / the one used in the past.

2 I don't think the museums in London are as interesting as the museums in Rome.
3 The museum's collection of medals isn't as good as the collection of coins.
4 I want to go there and no one is going to prevent me from going there.
5 I had always wanted to visit the Science Museum, and last week I visited the Science Museum.
6 'Will James come with us?' 'No, I don't think James will come with us.'

3 Speak

Work in groups of five. The following five places have been suggested for a school trip. Each student takes one of the places and argues why this should be chosen. Afterwards take a vote to decide.

- a local theme park (for example, Disneyworld)
- a science museum
- an art gallery
- a chocolate factory
- a national sporting event

4 Listen

a 🔊 Listen to a programme called *Our Heritage*.

1 What is the aim of the programme?
2 Which three of the things in the photographs are discussed in the programme?

b 🔊 Listen again and complete the notes in the table.

	Object one	Object two	Object three
When was it made?			
Name of object:			
Reason(s) for suggesting it:			

c If you could choose one of the three objects on the programme to go into the collection, which one would you choose?

5 Grammar

Ellipsis

a Ellipsis means 'leaving words out'. This happens quite often in English. Sentences 1–5 are things that people said in the programme. They are all shortened using ellipsis. What was left out? Choose the words which were left out from a–e.

1 Good to have you here.
2 Right, Mike.
3 Why choose a tin of tomatoes?
4 Might be a good idea.
5 Want to say anything else about it?

a did you
b It's
c It
d Do you
e You're

Look

This kind of ellipsis is something that is mostly done in informal, conversational situations.

b In each reply, one option is wrong (*W*), one is possible (*P*), one is the best (*B*). Say which is which.

1 A: Can you tell me how old it is?
  B: Yes, I   a can. *B*
           b can tell. *W*
           c can tell you. *P*

2 A: Are the tomatoes off?
  B: They   a might be off.
          b might be.
          c might.

3 A: Did you vote for the guitar?
  B: No, but if I'd known who to ring, I   a would.
                    b would have.
                    c would have voted.

4 A: Do you want to go to the cinema?
  B: Yes, I'd   a love to.
           b love.
           c love to go to the cinema.

5 A: Would you like to go for a walk?
  B: No thanks, I don't   a want.
                  b want to.
                  c want to go for a walk.

c Rewrite the dialogues. Leave out what you can in the answers.

1 A: Do you want to go out tonight?
  B: Yes, I'd love to go out tonight.

2 A: Do you think John has arrived?
  B: I'm not sure, but he might have arrived.

3 A: I don't want to go to the party.
  B: Why don't you want to go?
  A: Sally might be there.
  B: No, I don't think she will be there.

4 A: Is this the right answer?
  B: It might be the right answer. Why don't we ask Phil?
  A: No, I don't want to ask Phil.
  B: Why don't you want to ask him?

6 Vocabulary

Old and new

a Sentences 1–6 refer to things from the listening in Exercise 4. Can you remember what they are?

1 They can be more or less **contemporary**, or a little **old-fashioned**. *Items brought on to the show.*
2 I know it's **obsolete** technology now.
3 It isn't **out-of-date** yet.
4 That's certainly a **novel** idea!
5 It doesn't look **outdated**.
6 If you want **up to date** information on our show, don't forget to visit our website.

b Complete the definitions in the table with adjectives 1–6 from Exercise 6a. Use a dictionary if you need to.

old	new
outdated – old fashioned so not as good or useful as something modern; for example, machinery /weapons / ideas	.... – has a modern, 'today' feel to it, existing or happening now; for example, music / literature / art / fashion
.... – not modern, belonging to or typical of a time in the past; for example, clothes / ideas / furniture	.... – new and original, not like anything seen or heard of before, for example, ideas and suggestions
.... – describes food that is old and not now safe to eat; describes information that is old and not useful or correct; describes clothes, colours, styles that are old and not fashionable	.... – modern, recent, or containing the latest information; for example, database and news reports
.... – not in use any more, having been replaced by something newer and better or more fashionable	

c Work with a partner and discuss the questions.

1 Do you think your parents are old-fashioned? Explain your reasons.
2 Name three things that you think will be obsolete ten years from now. Explain your reasons.
3 What novel uses for old clothes can you think of?
4 What are the dangers of eating food which is out-of-date?
5 Which contemporary film stars do you like best?
6 100 years ago, many people believed 'Children should be seen and not heard'. What other outdated ideas from the past can you think of?

d Replace the words in italics in the sentences with a word from the box. You may need to change the words or add a word.

> update   renovate   restore   renew

1 The museum was really old, so they *repaired and improved* it completely.
2 The painting was in such bad condition that they were lucky to get it *back to its previous condition*.
3 That's the news so far – we'll *give you the latest information* during the rest of the day.
4 My library membership has run out – I'll have to *get a new version of* it.

e (Circle) the correct option.

1 He's one of the best *novel /(contemporary)* singers in the world.
2 I'm afraid I don't like those shoes – they look really *obsolete / outdated*.
3 They're trying to *renovate / restore* interest in sport in this country.
4 Keeping a sheep in the garden is a *novel / contemporary* way of keeping the grass short.
5 I want a new mobile phone – one that's *up-to-date / novel* with all the latest features.
6 Our school was falling to pieces, but it's been completely *renewed / renovated*.
7 You have to *renew / restore* your subscription to the magazine every two years.
8 I missed last week's meeting so I don't know what's happened – can you *update / restore* me please?

7 Speak

a Work in small groups. Together, your group chooses three items for *Our Heritage* and gives reasons why you have chosen them.

b Present your suggestions to your class.

c When everyone has presented, your class will vote together on the best five items to go into the collection.

Culture in mind

8 Read

(a) Read the text and answer the questions with *A* (Museum A), *B* (Museum B) or *C* (Museum C). According to the texts, which museum or museums:

1 restores old machines?
2 is located in a building of architectural interest?
3 has been on TV?
4 has had to change premises because it's become so popular?
5 houses objects from the famous?
6 can be visited on the Internet?

Museums – establishments dedicated to the preservation and maintenance of the world's finest treasures. But is this always the case? For every Louvre, there is a Museum of Bad Art, for every Natural History Museum there is one dedicated solely to the carrot. Welcome to the weird and wonderful world of alternative collections.

[A] Museum of Bad Art (MOBA), Boston, USA

The art on show in the MOBA collection consists of work from talented artists having a bad day to amateur painters who are 'barely in control of the brush.' Forget Da Vinci's *Mona Lisa* or Van Gogh's *Sunflowers*, for at MOBA you will only find the very worst the art world has to offer, paintings so truly awful that most people would have thrown them straight into the bin. Works such as the surrealist *In the cat's mouth* and Sandy Winslow's three eyed fluorescent portrait *More*. Since it was started in 1993, the museum has grown in reputation and size. It was originally housed in the basement of a private Boston home but the demand was so great that the permanent exhibition has now moved into the basement of a Boston theatre. There is also an online guide to exhibits so that all the world can sit back and admire, as the MOBA proudly advertises, 'art too bad to be ignored.'

[B] The British Lawnmower Museum, Southport, UK

In 1830 Edwin Beard Budding, who was working in a cotton mill in Stroud, Gloucestershire, invented a machine to cut cloth. He then had the idea to use it for cutting grass. People thought he was mad so he tested the machine at night so no one could see him. Nearly 200 years later, his invention, the lawnmower, is the subject of its very own museum.

Started by ex-racing champion Brian Radam, the British Lawnmower Museum attracts visitors from all over the world and offers a fascinating introduction into the history of every gardener's best friend.

From the mowers of the rich and famous (Prince Charles and Diana, Princess of Wales both included here) to a selection of some of the most expensive grass cutting machines ever built, the museum houses probably the largest collection of lawnmowers in the world. The museum also boasts some of the world's fastest machines which have been the feature of a TV programme.

The museum also has its own repair shop where you can get your mower fixed.

[C] The Bata Shoe Museum, Toronto, Canada

When does a love of shoes become an obsession? Perhaps when your collection reaches over 10,000 pairs. Luckily, Sonja Bata has decided to share her enthusiasm with the rest of the world and her enormous assortment of shoes, sandals and boots is now on display in architect Raymond Moriyama's award-winning four-storey building, which in itself is well worth the visit. Sonja, who is actively involved in the shoe industry, has been collecting shoes since the 1940s and has put together a fascinating collection that celebrates over 4,500 years of footwear history, including ancient Egyptian sandals, Chinese bound foot shoes (worn by woman to stop their feet from growing) and amazing psychedelic platform shoes from the 1970s. There is also a popular selection of shoes from the rich and famous in the 20th century. This includes shoes from icons such as John Lennon, Marilyn Monroe, Elizabeth Taylor and Picasso.

(b) Read the texts again. Match the names with the descriptions of each person.

1 Sandy Winslow   a He's used to life in the fast lane.
2 Edwin Beard Budding b Sharing her passion with the world.
3 Brian Radam   c So bad, he's almost good.
4 Sonja Bata   d They laughed at him until he proved them wrong.
5 Raymond Moriyama   e He designed a home for shoes.

(c) Work with a partner. Think of one question you would like to ask each of these people.

Discussion box

Work in pairs or small groups. Discuss these questions together.

1 Which of these museums would you like to visit most? Why?

2 Do you know of any other unusual museums? What are they like?

3 If you could open a museum, what would it be? Why?

9 Write

(a) Read the notes. Where do you think you might find each one?

1

Final reminder

Just to advice any students interested in going on a school trip to the Glasgow Transport Museum that they must give there names to Miss Chapel by Wednesday 3pm to insure a place. You will also need to have a consent from signed by a parent.

2

***** Lost *****

Has anyone found a pink iPod?

I think I probably left it on the bus that took us on the school trip to the museum last Saturday.

What a great trip that was. If you have found it, please contact Joe on 9897 2313.

3

You can't take photos.
Don't touch the things in the museum.
There's a good shop on your way out.

4

Hi Oliver,

I *called / have called* round to see if you wanted to come into town this afternoon. Me and Dave *are going / will go* CD shopping and we'll probably go to the cinema to see the *late / latest* Bond film later (*provided / unless* we've still got enough money, of course). I tried *to call / calling* your mobile but I *didn't / wasn't* manage to get through. Anyway, if you *do* want to come with us, give me a call on my mobile as soon as you can.

(b) Look back at the notices and answer the questions about each one.

1 Find and correct four spelling mistakes in note 1.

2 Which sentence is unnecessary in note 2?

3 Rewrite note 3 to make it more formal.

4 Circle the correct options in note 4. What essential piece of information is missing?

5 Rewrite note 5 to make it less formal.

(c) Read these guidelines for note writing. Which one do you think is not serious?

1 Keep your notes short. Do not include irrelevant information.

2 Make sure you include all the vital information.

3 Check your spelling and punctuation.

4 Always use blue or black ink when you write a note.

5 Use language that is appropriate to your target audience.

6 An attractive layout will help your note to be seen and read.

(d) Write notes for these situations.

1 You want to sell your laptop. Write a note to advertise it on the school notice board.

2 You have just passed your driving test. Write a note to thank your driving instructor.

3 You called at your friend's house to return some DVDs she lent you. She is not in. Write a note to leave on her door explaining what you have done with the films.

4 You are planning to put on a school play. Write a note looking for students who are interested in being in it or helping out with the production.

5 You are a cinema manager. Write some notes explaining different aspects of your policies.

5

Free to a good home.

We are in possession of six Labrador puppies, which we are willing to donate to anyone so wishing to own such a dog. Only those with a genuine love for the canine species will be considered.

Contact can be made by dialling 3433 3454 and then requesting to speak with Sue.

16 Swapping places

* Grammar review
* Vocabulary: teenspeak

1 Read and listen

a Look at the photos. Imagine you were at these shows. Write down five adjectives to describe your experience at each one. Compare your lists with a partner.

b 🔊 Read the text and write the numbers of the missing sentences in the spaces. Listen to check.

1 But I also had a sneaking suspicion that the whole act had been carefully choreographed.

2 and they explain to you how it is operated

3 My wife bought me a second-hand, outdoor table

4 The feeling was you could only appreciate high culture as long as you disdained popular culture

5 that's when people seem to make the transition

6 But I did find the music tough

7 But I wasn't sure if I would be able to appreciate the opera

8 He didn't like the music, but I didn't expect him to

Culture Shock

Charles Saumarez Smith, the director of the National Gallery, took his son Ferdinand to a French opera. In return, he was taken to see Iggy Pop and The Stooges.

FERDINAND: My father has always been more interested in classical stuff than me. At my age he was listening to classical music, not pop. I like all kinds of pop music, new stuff and also things back to the 1970s, which is why I wanted to take Dad to see Iggy Pop. My brother Otto introduced me to some bands, and I found the rest myself. **[A]**.

The court opera house in Sweden was built in 1766. We went behind the scenes; you can see all the eighteenth century stageworks **[B]**. It was a very long, very stylised production and the theatre was small and the benches hard and narrow. I found the scenery and costumes and the opera house itself the most interesting, it was a time capsule.

[C]. It might have been better if I hadn't started on such an intense opera. But it's an enthusiast's opera, so I don't see why they should make it accessible to kids. Even Dad, who is very knowledgeable, found the music pretty specialist. The main thing was that it was a nice day out, going to Sweden on a boat, seeing the opera house. I think I'll probably like classical music when I'm middle-aged, **[D]**.

I enjoyed taking Dad to see Iggy Pop. He had a great time, but I think he was a bit jealous of Iggy's hair and his

shape, given Iggy's seven years older. **[E]**. It was about him enjoying the showmanship. Afterwards we had a curry and sat up talking.

My brother and I have been educating Dad about pop music all summer. We played him Kraftwerk's Autobahn going over the Malmö bridge. I think we're doing quite a good job. The thing about my dad is that he's not a 'cool' dad, but he's a lot less stuffy than most people in museums. He recognises that people like unstuffy stuff so he's willing to open the gallery up to new things. At the National Portrait Gallery he did all sorts of different things, he even had portraits of pop stars like Blur.

CHARLES: I think it was impossible not to be caught up in the atmosphere. There was no one there when we arrived, but about 15 minutes before The Stooges came on about 4,000 people suddenly flowed in from nowhere.

For someone who is nearly 60, Iggy Pop is incredibly athletic and balletic. He was full of raw energy. It was impressive because it didn't feel like revival for the sake of revival, it had a vitality. **[F]**.

It was an experience, it was fun, but it was also true that a big part of the enjoyment was experiencing it with my sons. A bit of me occasionally feels that I should have tried out more diverse things when I was younger, but not much of me, I'm not the sort of person who is searching for his lost youth.

It is so interesting how attitudes to culture have changed. My parents and my school wanted me to appreciate culture, but it was always high culture; classical music, literature, theatre. **[G]**, if you listened to Schubert you couldn't bear to listen to The Rolling Stones.

It is much healthier now, you can pick and mix. I think my sons probably have more diverse cultural experiences to offer me than the other way round. I'm always interested to see how Ferdy and Otto engage in considerable depth with popular music and film; they are interested in the history of things. When I was younger you could only see the film that came to the local cinema once a week. But 'Sofa Cinema' is clearly a cultural revolution, you can find whatever you want from the past 80 years.

My wife and I have always been careful to let them follow their interests. Going to the opera was something my wife and I very much wanted to do, and I don't think it was quite Ferdy's thing: I suspect that 14 is just the age when you are least likely to follow your parents' interests.

We do, however, share some things. My current enthusiasm, more than opera, is for table tennis. **[H]** and I play with Ferdy in the evening after work. It satisfies my baser instincts: it's good exercise, but fiercely competitive. The main thing is it is a good game and it is something I can enjoy with my son.

c Read the text again and mark the statements *T* (true) or *F* (false). Correct the false statements.

1 Ferdinand's brother has helped influence Ferdinand's musical tastes. ☐

2 Ferdinand found the opera house more interesting than the opera itself. ☐

3 Ferdinand thought they should have made the opera easier for young people to understand. ☐

4 Ferdinand thinks his dad is quite open-minded for his age. ☐

5 Charles felt that Iggy Pop was exploiting his past reputation to make a bit more money. ☐

6 Both Ferdinand and Charles enjoyed being together more than the actual shows they went to. ☐

7 Charles regrets a bit that he didn't try out different things when he was younger. ☐

8 Charles thinks he can learn more culturally from his sons than they can from him. ☐

d Work with a partner. Find the words in the text and explain them in your own words.

1 it was a time capsule
2 The main thing
3 stuffy
4 flowed in
5 diverse
6 'Sofa Cinema'
7 influence
8 Ferdy's thing

Discussion box

Work in pairs or small groups. Discuss these questions together.

Imagine you had a similar experience with one of your relatives to Ferdinand and Charles in Exercise 1.

1 Who would you choose?
2 What would you make them do?
3 What do you imagine they would make you do?
4 What would you hope to achieve from the experience?

2 Grammar

Review

a Look at the missing sentences in Exercise 1b. Each one is an example of a structure you have studied in the book. Match the descriptions a–h with sentences 1–8 in Exercise 1b. Write in the boxes.

a adjective order ☐

b hedging ☐

c ability in the past ☐

d past perfect passive ☐

e ellipsis ☐

f a reporting verb ☐

g the emphatic auxiliary ☐

h conditional structure avoiding *if* ☐

b Work in two teams to complete the grammar revision quiz. Team A chooses a question for team B to answer, for example 4a. If team B gives the correct answer in 30 seconds they get a point. Then team B chooses a question for team A. Play until all questions have been answered correctly.

Grammar Quiz

1 Put the adjectives at the end of each sentence in the correct order.

  a We spent a morning on the beach. (Saturday / long / sunny)

  b He drives around in some car. (sports / expensive / Italian / red)

  c How much is that table under the window? (wooden / small / coffee / antique)

2 Put the words in order to make sentences.

  a to / appear / they / asleep / be

  b be / to / you / really / good / it's / for / believed

  c to / him / be / much / seems / than / last / he / time / older / I / saw / the

3 Correct the sentences.

  a I won't can make it to your party, I'm afraid.

  b The fire spread fast but we could escape just in time.

  c I might have could phone you if I knew your number.

4 Rewrite the sentences using the passive.

  a The thief had broken the window to escape.

  b She didn't know it but they had seen her.

  c The hurricane had destroyed the whole town.

5 ~~Cross out~~ the unnecessary words.

  a 'Do you want to come round for dinner tonight?'

  b 'Are you happy now?'

  c 'It's a nice day, isn't it?'

6 Rewrite the sentences using reported speech.

  a 'I didn't say anything,' he denied.

  b 'Are you ready to go?' she asked.

  c 'I didn't really like the film,' he admitted.

7 Rewrite the sentences to make them more emphatic. Use the words in brackets.

  a Paul told her, not me. (It)

  b He never said 'thank you' and I didn't like that. (What)

  c My dad sings in the shower. That's the embarrassing thing about him. (What)

8 'If we don't hurry, we'll miss the train.' Rewrite this sentence using:

  a as long as

  b unless

  c otherwise

9 Correct one word in each sentence.

  a Anya knew by now that it will be too cold to reach the summit of the mountain.

  b I was convinced I am going to win the quiz.

  c David was go to get a job in France next year, but he's decided not to.

10 Circle the correct answer.

  a In stressful situations, I often feel *like / liked* running away.

  b Kate's always *rush / rushing* from one place to another.

  c I think the constant pressure at work causes Ed *feeling / to feel* tired.

11 Write a sentence using *have something done* for each of the following.

  a my garden / redesign

  b my camera / repair

  c my car / clean

12 Rewrite each sentence using a negative inversion.

  a The contestants have to camp in a different place each night and hunt for food. (not only)

  b Susie left the party very shortly after she'd arrived! (no sooner)

  c Please don't eat or talk during this exam. (on no account)

3 Listen

(a) Work with a partner and discuss the questions.

1 Do you have arguments with your parents?
2 What kinds of things do you argue about?

(b) Work with a partner. Look at the photo from *Freaky Friday*. Student A is the mother. Write down five complaints you have about your daughter. Student B is the daughter. Write down five complaints you have about your mother. Tell each other your complaints.

(c) 🔊 Listen to a film review of *Freaky Friday*. Did the reviewer enjoy the film?

(d) 🔊 Listen again and answer the questions.

1 Why did the reviewer not want to see the film?
2 What made him change his mind?
3 What were the reviewer's previous opinions of Jamie Lee Curtis?
4 What do you learn about Jamie Lee Curtis's part in the film?
5 Why is the daughter in the film unhappy with her mother?
6 What aspect of each other's lives do they have to deal with when they switch bodies?
7 How do both actresses impress the reviewer?
8 What was the reviewer's one criticism of the film?

4 Vocabulary

Teenspeak

According to the reviewer one of the funniest parts of the film is hearing Jamie Lee Curtis using teenspeak. Here are some examples of the teenspeak in lines from the film. Match the underlined words in sentences 1–8 with the meanings a–h.

1 'Anna, your band Pink Slip is <u>da bomb</u>.'
2 'What do you think of Mr Bates' essay assignment?' '<u>Whatever</u>.'
3 'Mom, you're <u>totally</u> ruining my life.'
4 'That <u>biter</u> is wearing the same shirt I wore yesterday.'
5 'That kid's a <u>slacker</u>. He doesn't do his homework, ever.'
6 'Anna. Here's the <u>411</u>. Jake likes you and he's coming over here right now to talk to you.'
7 'Anna, you're so <u>busted</u>.'
8 'Mom, this shirt is <u>dorky</u>.'

a Let's talk about something else
b Someone who copies off you
c Someone who's lazy
d When someone gets caught doing something wrong
e All the information on a subject
f The ultimate in cool
g Weird, odd, not cool
h Completely, really, used to emphasis

5 Speak

Work with a partner and look at the quotations. Imagine what has had happened to each of these people to make them say these things.

'Janice probably argued a lot with her parents and thought that they were always wrong about everything. She's probably got teenagers herself now and realises that it's not always easy being the parent of a 16 year old.'

Things I wish I had known at 18.

'Sometimes parents are right.' – Janice 48

'Not to care so much what other people thought of me.' – Jules 32

'How to play the guitar.' – Rob 42

'Making money isn't everything.' – Lucy 28

'Appearances don't matter.' – Sally 32

'Take every day one at a time.' – Shaun 50

6 Song

(a) Write down four adjectives that you think describe your generation. Explain your list to your partner.

(b) 🔊 Listen to the song. Write down four adjectives to describe how the singer feels about his generation.

(c) 🔊 Listen again and complete the sentences with the words in the box.

> put (someone) down   get around   sensation   dig   fade away

My Generation by The Who

[Verse 1:]
People try to ¹_____ us _____ (Talking about my generation)
Just because we ²_____ _____ (Talking about my generation)
Things they do look awful cold (Talking about my generation)
I hope I die before I get old (Talking about my generation)

[Chorus:]
This is my generation
This is my generation, baby

[Verse 2:]
Why don't you all ³_____ _____ (Talking about my generation)
And don't try to ⁴_____ what we all say (Talking about my generation)
I'm not trying to cause a big ⁵_____ (Talking about my generation)
I'm just talking about my generation (Talking about my generation)

[Chorus:]
This is my generation
This is my generation, baby

[Repeat verse 2]

[Chorus:]
This is my generation
This is my generation, baby

[Repeat verse 1]

(d) Match the missing words from the song with definitions 1–5.

1   disappear
2   do a lot of things
3   understand
4   criticise
5   impression

(e) What is the singer's message and who is it to? Write a short paragraph to explain it.

Did you know ...?

Known for their explosive, power rock, The Who are considered by many to be the greatest British rock band of all time – better than both The Beatles and The Stones. They have had a huge influence on many artists such as Oasis, Blur and Paul Weller.

The Who enjoyed their biggest success during the late 1960s, when they were part of the London Mod scene, and also when they wrote the rock opera Tommy. However, the two surviving members of the original line up, Roger Daltrey and Pete Townshend, continue to record and tour today.

7 Write

(a) Work with a partner. Read the common proverbs and then discuss the questions.

1. *A bad excuse is better than none.*

2. *A bird in the hand is worth two in the bush.*

3. *A bad workman blames his tools.*

4. *Rome wasn't built in a day.*

5. *Children and fools tell the truth.*

6. *He who laughs last, laughs longest.*

7. *He who hesitates is lost.*

8. *Fish and guests smell in three days.*

9. *Tomorrow never comes.*

1. What do you think the proverbs mean?
2. Think of a real example to illustrate one.
3. Do you agree with them?

(b) Meaningless proverbs are a new type of word play. To write them you take the beginning of one proverb and the ending of another, and put the two together so that you create a new and meaningless saying. Here is a list of proverbs. Which two proverbs in Exercise 7a were used to create the meaningless one below?

A bad workman wasn't built in a day.

(c) Now use some of the other proverbs to create your own meaningless proverbs. Read them out in class and try and explain why they might make sense.

'A bad workman wasn't built in a day'. This means that just as we have to learn how to do things properly, we can also learn how to do things badly too. We're not born doing things wrong.

(d) The word *cinquain* is French, and means a grouping of five. The cinquain has five lines, with two, four, six, eight, and two syllables – so 22 syllables altogether. Read the cinquains. Work with a partner and discuss who could have written each one and why? Use your imagination.

Silence.
No single word?
Why can't you and I talk?
It doesn't have to be like this.
Trust me.

Nature
Source of beauty
Refreshing relaxing
Sitting on top of the mountain
Breathe it

(e) Choose a topic and write your own cinquain.

For your portfolio

Unit 16   113

✱ Module 4 Check your progress

1 Grammar

(a) Put the verb in the correct tense. Choose the future perfect or the future continuous.

1 This time next week, I .... (finish) all my exams and I'll be free for the summer holidays.

This time next week, I will have finished all my exams and I'll be free for the summer holidays.

2 I .... (do) a test from 9am to 10am, so don't phone my mobile then.

3 When I finish this one, I .... (read) three books this week.

4 I .... (fix) my bike this Sunday morning if you want to come round and help me.

5 We .... (leave) for the party around 9pm so if you want a lift, get here before then.

6 Phone me at 6pm. I .... (find) the problem by then and I'll tell you how much it'll be to fix.

7 When we come back from Chile next year, I .... (visit) all seven continents.

8 We .... (sing) 'Happy Birthday' around 5pm so please be home by then.

| 7 |

(b) <u>Underline</u> the correct option to complete the sentences.

1 He's getting really angry and is *about to / due to* lose his temper.

2 I'm just *off to / supposed to* the shops. I won't be long.

3 The final's *due to / bound to* take place in the new stadium – if it's finished on time.

4 Knowing my luck, I'm *thinking of failing / bound to fail* my driving test again.

5 We're *off to / supposed to* give the essay in on Friday. I'll never finish it by then.

6 I'm *thinking of taking / bound to take* a year off to travel around Europe before university, but I'm not sure yet.

7 We're *supposed to / about to* get the results on Tuesday. I'm really nervous.

8 He's *bound to / off to* Australia next month to start a new life.

| 7 |

(c) Rewrite the sentences using the beginning given.

1 It's a shame I didn't study harder at school.

If only *I had studied harder at school.*

2 My sister keeps taking my clothes without asking. It really annoys me.

I wish ....

3 Let's give our money to charity this year instead of going on holiday.

I'd rather we ....

4 Why don't you stop complaining about it and do something.

It's time ....

5 I'd love to buy a new car but I haven't got enough money.

If only ....

6 Why did I say that? I must have sounded so stupid!

I wish ....

7 It's a secret so don't tell her.

I'd rather you ....

8 I think we need to sit down and talk about it.

It's time ....

| 7 |

(d) Rephrase the underlined parts of these sentences.

1 He always said he would win the race and yesterday he <u>won it</u>.

He always said he would win the race and yesterday he did so.

2 'Is he French?' 'No, I <u>don't think he's French</u>.'

3 I like the beaches in Bali better than <u>the beaches</u> in Australia.

4 She didn't want to go to the party and <u>her brother didn't want to go to the party either</u>.

5 His paintings of nature are better than <u>his paintings</u> of people.

6 I wanted to visit him in hospital but his mother stopped me from <u>visiting him there</u>.

7 The police do an important job: <u>the job of</u> keeping law and order on the streets.

8 My parents want to go to Indonesia next holiday and <u>I want to go there too</u>.

| 7 |

e) Find and correct the mistakes in each of the sentences.

1   He's just bought an Italian antique fantastic cabinet.
   He's just bought a fantastic, antique Italian cabinet.

2   I don't really know him. He seems being a bit shy.

3   When we got home we found the house had been being broken into.

4   I didn't think the film was very good and so did my friend.

5   He denied to having lied to me.

6   It's the way she speaks to me what I find most annoying.

7   Unless he doesn't apologise, I won't talk to him again.

8   It was a difficult test but I could pass it.

   [ ][7]

2 Vocabulary

a) Match the sentence halves.

1   My older brother had to take
2   It took me five years to pay
3   My dad's taken
4   I'm not going to start
5   I don't feel I'm ready to settle
6   I think I'd like to change
7   I really regret dropping
8   I want to leave

a   off my university loans.
b   a family until I'm at least 30.
c   down yet.
d   careers at least once in my life.
e   out a loan to pay for his university course.
f   out of school so early.
g   early retirement. He's only 55.
h   school as soon as I can.

    [7]

b) Circle the correct options. Check with the text.

1   The university has *raised* / *risen* its fees again.

2   Be careful what you say to him. He's quite *sensible* / *sensitive* about the whole issue.

3   The exact *effect* / *affect* of the war on the people will never be known.

4   Have you got any *advise* / *advice* on what internet provider I should use?

5   Ask her. She can only say 'no'. I mean, what have you got to *lose* / *loose*?

6   You'll have to *ensure* / *insure* yourself if you want to drive my car.

7   If you're not feeling very well, you should go and *lie* / *lay* down for a few minutes.

8   They hadn't got enough evidence so he couldn't be *prosecuted* / *persecuted*.

   [ ][7]

c) Complete the sentences with the words in the box.

> novel   out-of-date   restore
> renew   update   ~~obsolete~~
> old-fashioned   renovated

1   I can't believe you still listen to CDs. That technology is almost *obsolete* . Get an MP3 player.

2   That's a _____ idea. It's very original.

3   We got the house really cheaply because it needs to be _____ quite a bit.

4   My passport is _____ so I can't travel anywhere.

5   There's been a bit of damage to the legs but I think we can _____ this table to its former glory.

6   The police don't have much information at the moment but have promised to _____ us as soon as they know more.

7   I've got to go to the gym and _____ my membership.

8   I wear a lot of my grandmother's old clothes. You might think they'd be a bit _____ but they're not.

   [ ][7]

How did you do?

Tick (✓) a box for each section.

Total score:	☺	☹	☹
[ ] 56	Very good	OK	Not very good
Grammar	27 – 35	18 – 26	less than 18
Vocabulary	16 – 21	10 – 15	less than 10

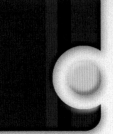

Writing bank 1
Formal letters/emails

1 Model letter

(a) Read the model letter. What is the writer's main complaint?

Starting the letter / email
Dear Sir or Madam / Dear Mr / Ms / Mrs [X]

Opening phrases
I am writing in response to … / The reason I am writing is to … I am writing with reference to / with regard to / concerning

Referring to a new topic
With regard to [X], … / Where …

Dear Sirs

I am writing to comment on the article in your magazine last week about 'English plus Tourism' packages sold through IQ language programmes. Whereas you seem to have a positive impression of what IQ have to offer, it is my opinion that their packages leave a lot to be desired.

I bought a package with IQ last year, and found that the gap between what was offered and what I received to be substantial. For example, the package stated that I would be met at London airport and taken 'speedily to Bulgrove College', (the location of the language course). My plane landed at 2 pm after an 11 hour flight. The IQ representative explained that several other people on the course would 'be landing soon', and I was asked to wait. To cut a long story short, I had to wait until almost 7 pm until everyone had arrived, and we were then put on a coach for the transfer to Bulgrove eventually arriving 10 o'clock. This, in my opinion, is an interesting definition of the word 'speedily'.

As far as accommodation at the college was concerned, it was not up to the standard suggested in the advert. My room was tiny, and the 'en-suite' bathroom had no heating – something that I would have thought is essential during an English winter. The writing desk was very small, which made working in the evening less comfortable than it could have been. Moreover, the promised wi-fi connection in the room often didn't work. Naturally, I complained; but the Bulgrove staff appeared indifferent, and certainly no action was taken.

I would like to point out that the teaching I received was excellent. The main objective of the trip was to learn more English, and mine unquestionably improved. On the other hand, I spent two weeks in poor and cramped accommodation which simply was not worth the money charged.

On my return home, I wrote to IQ and raised these points. Not surprisingly, they have never bothered to reply.

Overall, my experience leads me to suggest to your readers that they think twice before signing up for an IQ course.

Yours faithfully

P. Mendonça

Giving opinions
I would have though that … / To my min… / From my point view …

Making points clea
I wish to make it cle… / It's important t… say that …

Finishing the letter email
Yours sincerely (if y begin the letter usi the person's name, example, Dear Mr Smith) / Yours faithfully (if you be the letter with, for example, Dear Sirs)

Closing phrases
I would like to end by saying … / May I close by [saying] ….

(b) Look at the phrases in the boxes. Rewrite each of the underlined phrases in the letter with an expression from the relevant box.

Style tips for formal letters/emails

- Use the full forms of verbs (for example *is not* rather than *isn't*, *cannot* rather than *can't*, etc.)
- Use a wide range of grammatical structures if you can. Be as impressive as possible!
- Use formal register (for example, *Furthermore / However / Naturally / a further opportunity / enormous experience / we have no objection to … / We would be delighted to …*)
- Avoid the use of phrasal verbs, for example use *discover* rather than *find out*
- When criticising, avoid bold statements and use hedging words like *tend / may / seem / appear* (for example, instead of *He didn't realise this*, you can say *He appears not to have realised this*.)
- Use boosting devices to make your own points stronger (for example, *It is undoubtedly the case that … / This is unquestionably …*)

2 Task

Choose one of the following tasks. Write between 200 and 250 words.

- You read a negative magazine review of a film that you enjoyed. You also feel the review includes incorrect information. Write a letter to the magazine to say how and why you disagree with the review.
- A student is coming on an exchange programme to spend six months in your school. Your school principal has asked you to write a letter of welcome to the student, including any useful information and advice you think necessary.

For your portfolio

Writing bank 2
Informal letters/emails

1 Model letter

a Read the model letter. What are the writer's plans?

● ● ○

Hi Paolo,
Just thought I'd drop you a quick line since I haven't been in touch for a while.

Guess what? I've decided to take a year off between school and university (a 'gap year' is what they call it here) so I can see a bit of the world and get some real-life experience before I head back to more studying! I wasn't sure that my parents would back me up, but in fact they're right behind me. Mind you, they're pretty keen that I should use the time constructively.

So here's what I think I'll do. I'll spend the three or four months working – you know, any old job that pays reasonably well. Actually, I'll get more than one job if I can. I'm thinking of maybe working in a shop during the day and then doing something in a restaurant in the evenings and weekends if I can, washing up or whatever. So I'll save up loads and then head off.

What I want to do first is some volunteer work for about six months. I've heard of an organisation that sends people to West Africa to help out on building projects, you know, things where you don't need specialised knowledge, you can just help with muscle power! So I'll do that for a while, and then take the last month or so travelling and holidaying somewhere.

Which brings me to the 'somewhere' bit! I'm thinking of travelling back across Europe and that includes Italy. Any chance of staying with you for a little while (a couple of weeks or so) next July or August? It'd be great to see you again and find out a bit about Italian life.

Anyway, when you have a spare moment, let me know if I can stay with you. Here's hoping that all's well with you – drop me a line sometime, please, and let me know your news.

Take care and all the best
Alex

Style tips for informal letters/emails

- Use simple sentence structure.
- Use informal register (for example, *a bit / pretty [keen] / any old [job] / or whatever*)
- Use simple linking words (for example, *So / Anyway / Actually / you know / Mind you / Then / After that / Well*)
- Use contracted forms (for example, *I'll save ..., not I will save ...*)
- Use phrasal verbs when you can (for example *back me up* rather than *support me*)
- Use vague language (for example, *about / or so / roughly / a bit / or whatever / stuff like that*)
- Use brackets when you add some not very important information (for example, *a couple of weeks, perhaps*)

b Write the words / phrases in the box in the correct column.

> Keep in touch
> Let me know how you are
> Take care   How's life?
> I reckon
> Sorry I haven't written for a while

Starting the letter / email	Dear [X] / Hello [X] / Hi [X]
Opening phrases	1 _____ / How are things with you? / Hope you're well / Just thought I'd drop you a (quick) line / 2 _____
Introducing topics	Guess what? I wanted to tell you that ... / Have you heard about ... ?
Giving opinions	3 _____ / The way I see it / If you ask me / I'd have thought
Closing phrases	Hope to hear from you soon / 4 _____ / Drop me a line sometime soon / Looking forward to hearing from you / Hope you're well / 5 _____ / Send me news
Finishing the letter / email	6 _____ / All the best / Best wishes / Love / Lots of love / Cheers

2 Task

Choose one of the following tasks. Write between 200 and 250 words.

- Imagine you are Paolo. Write a reply to Alex's letter. Give your news and reply to the request.
- Imagine you are Alex. You have started your volunteer work in West Africa. Write another letter/email to Paolo to give him your news.

For your portfolio

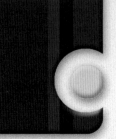

Writing bank 3
Narratives

1 Model story

a Read the model story. How did the divers feel after they had seen the whale shark?

A creature from a different world

A sharp gust of wind whipped rain into my face. Our tiny boat was ploughing through choppy waves across the Indian Ocean and I was absolutely freezing. The further we got from the shelter of the land, the more I thought how foolish I'd been to come along on this trip. Why hadn't I listened to my sensible friends? They'd be enjoying themselves back on the island – lazing around, and laughing about me, gullible enough to believe the diving instructor's promise of 'almost guaranteed' sightings of whale sharks.

The pilot of the boat, a small craft called a *dhoni*, was a local who didn't speak a word of English. He looked almost 60 but, perhaps because of a lifetime on the open sea in the hot sun, was remarkably fit and strong. I was wondering how he managed to find his way. To me, it seemed difficult enough to navigate a boat without any electronic equipment even on a sunny day. But it was a mystery to me how he could know where he was on a day with hardly any visibility at all. He seemed so aware and capable, even though he seemed to be steering his *dhoni* into the middle of absolutely nowhere.

So at least we were safe. But this was not what we had come along for. A look at the other divers' faces suggested that now they were also doubtful that we'd ever get the chance to see a whale shark – these weather conditions were totally unsuitable for diving! None of us spoke. It seemed too much of an effort. Then suddenly the boatman stopped the engine. <u>He said a few words in his own language to the diving instructor, who immediately jumped up from his seat and told us to get ready to dive. Despite my doubts, I hurried to get my gear on. Regulator open, check the pressure – weights, tank, flippers, mask. Ready? Okay!</u>

When I plunged into the grey sea, I was sure I wouldn't see anything. But then … there it was! An enormous whale shark, slowly gliding through the water. I couldn't believe my eyes – my first whale shark! What a beautiful sight! I hardly dared breathe – I was afraid my streams of bubbles might scare the gigantic creature away. And the other divers were equally awed. Slowly we approached this majestic animal … it could have come from a different world, it seemed so unreal. It was swimming quite slowly and we were able to swim with it, looking at the beautiful markings on its back. I was still holding my breath, telling myself that this huge fish was harmless! Then I reached out and touched it, stroking its thick skin. It was amazing how this giant suddenly gained speed – we watched it disappear, and a few moments later it was gone in the expanses of the ocean.

Less than an hour later, in the boat on the way back to the island, how different the mood among the divers was. We were all thrilled by what we had seen, and we were amazed how the boatman had actually been able to take us right up to a whale shark. How on earth had he been able to do that? Luck?

Coincidence? Instinct? We had no idea, and it didn't really matter. What did matter was the fact that we'd all had the most exciting diving experience ever!

Style tips for narratives

- Use the opening paragraph to get the reader's attention. Do not just report the facts, but describe the setting of the story, and add in some details that make it easier for the reader to imagine what the situation was like.
- In the following two or three paragraphs, describe how the story unfolds. Use adjectives and adverbs to make your narration more imaginative. Use varied vocabulary and sentence structure. Don't forget to help the reader understand the protagonists' emotions.
- To create tension, change the rhythm of the language by sometimes using long sentences and sometimes very short ones. (But make sure that your sentences are not <u>too</u> long!) Look at the extract underlined in the story as an example.
- In the final paragraph, round off the story. Say what the experience meant to you personally.

b Rewrite these examples. Use the style tips above to help you.

1 **Opening paragraph**
Rachel prepared everything for the party. All the family were coming. That would be nice. The weather was good which was nice.

2 **Following paragraph**
The guests arrived and talked to each other. They ate the food. They listened to music. Some guests laughed a lot. Some guests were quiet.

3 **Paragraph to create tension**
Rachel had prepared a cake for her grandmother and her small baby daughter crawled to the table and looked at it and put her hand in it and the whole cake collapsed.

4 **Final paragraph**
The party lasted for six hours. All the food was eaten. Everyone enjoyed it a lot.

2 Task

Choose one of the following ideas. Write a 200–250-word story.

- A fantastic trip you once had on holiday.
- An exciting moment in your own life.
- A frightening moment in your own life.
- Your first day at a new job / holiday job / college

For your portfolio

Writing bank 4
Discursive compositions

1 Model composition

(a) Read the composition. What is the writer's view on 'stars' of reality TV?

> **There should be laws protecting famous people from the paparazzi. Discuss.**
>
> On August 31st 1997 Diana, Princess of Wales was killed in a high speed car chase in Paris. Her driver had been trying to escape from press photographers. After the sorrow and sadness came the outrage. For a while, the paparazzi were more unpopular than traffic wardens and tax inspectors. Then came the debate; did we need to protect our rich and famous and ensure nothing like this happened again, or should things remain as they were so that glossy magazines could continue to fill their pages with popular photos of celebrities?
>
> First and foremost we should remember that, despite all their fame, celebrities are people just like the rest of us. They deserve privacy and the right to lead their own lives away from the camera. Constant press intrusion is at best a nuisance. At worst, it can make a life a misery. And let's not forget that it might also be the family of the celebrity who end up leading a miserable life, too. Moreover, there is something distasteful about groups of photographers running down a street behind a car, shouting and jostling for the best angle. And of course, when they pursue their victims by car, the result can be tragic – as was the case of Princess Diana.
>
> On the other hand, there is the argument that without the paparazzi many of these people would be forgotten, for example the 'stars' of reality TV shows. Many 'stars' become well-known for their private lives rather than their professional capabilities. Paris Hilton appears to be famous only because of generous coverage in the glossy magazines of her social life. Furthermore, many of these celebrities seem very happy to have the press around when they are trying to promote their careers. In other words, you can't have your cake and eat it too.
>
> Finally we should remember that fame brings responsibilities. Most famous people serve as role models to large sections of society, especially the young. Consequently, celebrities need to think carefully about their behaviour and whether or not it sets a good example. By setting a good example, they may find the paparazzi are more respectful towards their privacy.
>
> To sum up, I believe that in our private lives, we all have the right to do what we want, within reason. Therefore I think there should be a law that protects everyone from this kind of invasion of privacy. Having said that, I do not believe we can stop the paparazzi from taking photos once those stars step out into the world. I believe that the stars themselves need to think how they behave in public and use the press to their own advantage. A quick wave and smile for the camera hurts no one.

Style tips for discursive compositions

- Give points supporting both sides of the argument. Raise the arguments that you don't agree with, then show why you think they are wrong. Keep to the facts.
- Plan four stages; an introduction, arguments for (or against), arguments against (or for) and a conclusion.
- Quotations and real-life examples are good ways of starting your text.
- Be careful not to be repetitive. Vary your use of verbs (*I believe, I think, It seems …*)

(b) Write the words / phrases in the box in the correct column.

> consequently   in other words
> whereas   on the other hand
> since   to sum up   furthermore
> first and foremost

Beginning	*firstly, to begin with,* 1 _____ , *in the first place*
Giving reasons	*because (of), as, in response to,* 2 _____ , *so that*
Contrasting comparing	*however, although, despite,* 3 _____ , *in contrast to,* 4 _____ , *having said that*
Adding points	*and,* 5 _____ , *moreover,* *what's more, finally*
Talking about consequence	*as a result of,* 6 _____ , *and so, therefore*
Paraphrasing	7 _____ , *to put it another* *way, that is to say,*
Concluding	8 _____ , *in conclusion,* *when all's said and done*

2 Task

Choose one of the titles and write a 200–250-word composition.

- Global warming is the biggest threat to the safety of our planet. Discuss.
- The minimum age for driving should be raised to 21. Discuss.

For your portfolio

Writing bank 5
News reports

1 Model report

a) Read the model report and find out how many times Finnish men have won the competition.

Finns keep up the heat in Sauna championships

A FINNISH MAN and a Belarussian woman have been crowned king and queen of the sauna [1]_____ winning the world sauna endurance titles last Sunday.

Former three time champion Leo Pusa spent nearly 12 minutes in the scorching 110°C temperatures [2]_____ , reclaimed the title he had lost the previous year to a fellow countryman. In the women's event Natalya Tryfanava from Belarus won her second title in as many years [3]_____ managing to stay in the sauna for eight minutes.

The annual competition takes place in the Finnish town Heinola, 130km north of Helsinki. This was the sixth year of the championships [4]_____ this year saw twelve countries supplying ninety competitors.

The athletes sit in specially constructed saunas on a big stage. Water is added onto the coals every half a minute [5]_____ ensure that temperatures are kept stable. [6]_____ contestants can no longer bear the heat they rush out of the sauna (and the competition) [7]_____ to cool down. The action is followed by several thousand fans [8]_____ watch the proceedings on a giant video screen.

Tryfanava said that her team (Belarus also won third and fourth place in the women's competition) had undergone special training for this year's contest [9]_____ refused to give any more details.

The Finns have never lost the men's title [10]_____ it is hard to see them being beaten in the near future. In a country with a population of five million there are over two million saunas.

Linking ideas

b) Complete the text with the words below.

and in doing so	in order	when
which	to	but	after	who
by	and		

Style tips for reports and articles

- The main aim of a news report is to pass on information to the reader. Before you start, make sure you have all the facts. Then you should concentrate on how you can best present them in way which will hold your reader's interest.
- A good report starts with a quick summary of the story. It presents the most important information. It should make the reader want to read on to find out more about the story.
- Then the report should go over the background to the story adding more details to the facts presented in the opening paragraph.
- Most news reports ask to be taken seriously, therefore quite formal language is normally used when writing them. However, this is not always the case. Some newspapers are famous for using informal language in order to make their reports more sensational. Before you start writing, think of your audience and ask yourself what style of writing they would appreciate most.
- Finally, a news report needs a good headline – something to attract the reader's eye and make them want to read it.

2 Task

Write a report (200–250 words) on some local news for the school newspaper. Choose one of the following ideas.

- An exciting sports event
- A local charity event
- A trip of a lifetime
- An act of heroism

Writing bank 6
Notes and notices

1 Model notes and notices

(a) Read the model notes/notices. Which note might you find:

1 on a fridge door?
2 on a school notice board?
3 in a shop window?
4 in the 'classified ads' section of a newspaper?

WANTED

Sales assistants. £6/hr
pt or ft positions
Mon - Sat
Apply within

Party this Friday

It's the end of term
so let's celebrate.

Fun starts at eight – Don't be late

Book your place with Sue
(secretary)

BYOB (non-alcoholic only!)

For sale
Dawes 10 speed
mountain bike.
Ex cond
£250 obo
Phone 2323 2343

Jake – Read this!!!!!!!
Bob called about the footie
tomorrow.
Is it still on? Phone him asap.

Style tips for notes and notices

- Be brief. People don't generally expect to spend a long time reading a notice. If a notice contains a lot of text, it won't attract many readers.
- Don't forget to include all the important points. There's no use being brief if you don't get your message across. The secret of writing an effective note is how to include the essential information as efficiently as possible.
- Think about where you are going to display your note/notice. This might affect the way you write it. In a newspaper you'll probably have to think carefully about the number of words you use. If your notice is to put on a wall, you will want to think about using different colours and letter sizes to attract attention.
- Check your spelling and grammar. Even though notes/notices are often fairly informal, bad spelling and grammatical mistakes will create a bad impression.
- Use a good heading. This is what will attract your readers. It should tell them what to expect.

(b) Look at these headings and match them with the types of note/notice.

1	Wanted	a	I am selling ...
2	For sale	b	I am giving away ...
3	Lost	c	This is the final time I'm going to say this.
4	Found	d	We want to advise you about a dangerous situation.
5	Free to a good home	e	I have found ...
6	Last reminder	f	I am looking for ...
7	Warning	g	I am interested in buying ...

(c) We often use abbreviations in notes/notices. Look back at the model texts and find the abbreviations for:

1 part-time ....
2 excellent condition ....
3 as soon as possible ....
4 or best offer ....
5 all week ....
6 per hour ....
7 full-time ....
8 bring your own bottle ....
9 football ....

2 Task

Write notes for the following situations.

1 You are looking for a room to rent in a house.
2 You want to sell your laptop.
3 Your dog has had puppies and you want to give them away.
4 You have found a wallet and want to return it.

Pronunciation exercises

Unit 2
Sounding polite or angry

(a) 🔊 Listen to the phrases. What do you think each speaker will say next? ⬭Circle⬭ the correct option.

1 Perhaps you could tell me
a why you're late again.
b a little bit about yourself.
2 I don't really know what to tell you,
a I'm very, very disappointed.
b I've never really thought about it before.
3 Just give me a moment, OK.
a I'll be with you as soon as I can.
b You're not the only person who needs me, you know.
4 Would you mind if I asked you
a not to talk when I'm talking, OK?
b where you bought that lovely coat?

(b) 🔊 Listen and check. Practise saying each sentence in the same way.

(c) 🔊 Practise saying the sentences politely or angrily. Your partner guesses how you are feeling.

1 Perhaps you could tell me why you did that.
2 I don't really know what to tell you except I'm sorry.

3 Just give me a moment, OK. I'm busy
4 Would you mind if I asked you where you're going?

Unit 6
Stress in phrases

(a) Read the phrases. Which parts do you think are stressed? Underline the stressed words / syllables.

1 again and again and again
2 Off we went.
3 Would you believe it?
4 All of a sudden ...
5 That was the amazing thing.
6 What happened in the end?

(b) 🔊 Listen and check. Then listen again and repeat.

(c) Practise saying these phrases. Think about the stress you use.

1 that reminds me
2 and before we knew it ...
3 you know what it's like
4 a few minutes later
5 no matter what we did
6 we couldn't believe our eyes

Unit 10
Linking sounds

(a) 🔊 Listen to these phrases being said. How are the underlined parts said?

1 as it happens ...
2 as a matter of interest

3 To sum up, ...
4 So, going back to what I was saying ...
5 can you just bear with me?
6 the first thing I want to say

(b) 🔊 Listen again and repeat

(c) 🔊 Read the phrases aloud. Note how you join the words together, and try to read each phrase without pausing at all. Then listen and compare.

1 I hope I've managed to make it clear.
2 They designed the city to look like a plane.
3 There are some great things to do in our town.
4 This is what I'm going to talk about today.

Unit 14
Stress and intonation

(a) 🔊 Mark the stressed words. Listen and check.

1 The thing is, ...
2 On the other hand, ...
3 Tell you what, ...
4 To be honest, ...
5 To tell you the truth, ...
6 We're going round in circles.

(b) 🔊 Listen and repeat the phrases. Note how the speaker's voice goes up or down at the end of the phrase.

Phonetic symbols

Consonants						
/p/	pen	/m/	make	/j/	you
/b/	be	/n/	nice	/h/	he
/t/	two	/ŋ/	sing	/θ/	thing
/d/	do	/s/	see	/ð/	this
/k/	can	/z/	trousers	/ʃ/	she
/g/	good	/w/	we	/tʃ/	cheese
/f/	five	/l/	listen	/ʒ/	usually
/v/	very	/r/	right	/dʒ/	German

Vowels			
/æ/	man	/uː/	food
/ɑː/	father	/ʌ/	up
/e/	ten	/ɒ/	hot
/ɜː/	thirteen	/ɔː/	four
/ə/	mother		
/ɪ/	sit		
/iː/	see		
/ʊ/	book		

Diphthongs	
/eɪ/	great
/aɪ/	fine
/ɔɪ/	boy
/ɪə/	hear
/eə/	chair
/aʊ/	town
/əʊ/	go
/ʊə/	pure

Speaking exercises: extra material

Unit 4, page 27, Exercise 7

Student B: Look at picture B and imagine you are the person in
the picture. Describe your situation to Student A.

Unit 6, page 43, Exercise 5

Student B: Here is the outline of an urban legend. You have five
minutes to think of more details for it and make it as convincing
as possible. Then you must tell Student A the story. Student A
has to decide if it is true or not.

> You saw this in an email.
>
> The planet Mars is moving towards Earth.
>
> In the year 2060 it will be closer to Earth than ever before.
>
> This will change the tides and the electrical charges around Earth.
>
> Aeroplanes will have problems flying, and there will be other problems too.

* Wordlist

(v) = verb   (n) = noun   (adj) = adjective   (adv) = adverb

Unit 1

Animals sounds

bark (v) /baːk/
bleat (v) /bliːt/
crow (v) /krəʊ/
grunt (v) /grʌnt/
hiss (v) /hɪs/
roar (v) /rɔː/
squeak (v) /skwiːk/

Nouns

anecdote /ˈænɪkdəʊt/
behaviour /bɪˈheɪvjə/
breed /briːd/
cadence /ˈkeɪdəns/
chameleon /kəˈmiːliən/
cricket /ˈkrɪkɪt/
elephant handler /ˈelɪfənt ˈhændlə/
feat /fiːt/
Golden Retriever /ˈgəʊldən rɪˈtriːvə/
Jack Russell /dʒæk ˈrʌsl/
mode /məʊd/
no matter what the odds /nəʊ ˈmætə wɒt ðiː ɒdz/
pack of wolves /pæk ɒv wʊlvz/
peril /ˈperəl/
playpen /ˈpleɪpen/
predator /ˈpredətə/
retrogression /ˌretrʊˈgreʃən/
shark /ʃaːk/
silkworm /ˈsɪlkwɜːm/
sixth sense /sɪksθ sens/
sledge dog /sledʒ dɒg/
teeth marks /tiːθ maːks/
tissue /ˈtɪʃuː/
vibration /vaɪˈbreɪʃən/
warning signal /ˈwɔːnɪŋ ˈsɪgnəl/
warning system /ˈwɔːnɪŋ ˈsɪstəm/

Verbs

abandon /əˈbændən/
acclaim /əˈkleɪm/
bolt /bəʊlt/
burst into flames /bɜːst ˈɪntə fleɪmz/
calm (someone) down /kaːm daʊn/
carry (something) out /ˈkæri aʊt/
detect /dɪˈtekt/
emerge /ɪˈmɜːdʒ/
evacuate /ɪˈvækjueɪt/

honour /ˈɒnə/
howl /haʊl/
precede /priːˈsiːd/
race off /reɪs ɒf/
reason (something) out /ˈriːzən aʊt/
run (something) down /ˈrʌn daʊn/
sense /sens/
snatch (someone) up /snætʃ ʌp/
tag /tæg/

Adjectives

agitated /ˈædʒɪteɪtɪd/
canine /ˈkeɪnaɪn/
countless /ˈkaʊntləs/
earthquake-prone /ˈɜːθkweɪk prəʊn/
erratic /ɪˈrætɪk/
geological /ˌdʒɪəˈlɒdʒɪkl/
indifferent /ɪnˈdɪfərənt/
indigestible /ˌɪndɪˈdʒestəbəl/
keen /kiːn/
loathsome /ˈləʊðsəm/
numerous /ˈnjuːmərəs/
peculiar /pɪˈkjuːliə/
revered /rɪˈvɪəd/
sceptical /ˈskeptɪkəl/
sharp /ʃaːp/
snug /snʌg/
stout /staʊt/
supposed /səˈpəʊzd/
unfed /ʌnˈfed/

Adverbs

cunningly /ˈkʌnɪŋli/
electronically /ˌɪlekˈtrɒnɪkli/
precisely /prɪˈsaɪsli/
remarkably /rɪˈmaːkəbli/
secretly /ˈsiːkrətli/

Unit 2

Making decisions

dither (v) /ˈdɪðə/
informed decision (n) /ɪnˈfɔːmd dɪˈsɪʒən/
jump to the wrong conclusion (v) /dʒʌmp tuː ðə rɒŋ kənˈkluːʒən/
make (your) mind up (v) /meɪk jə maɪnd ʌp/
mull (something) over (v) /mʌl ˈəʊvə/
snap decision (n) /snæp dɪˈsɪʒən/

split-second decision (n) /splɪt ˈsekənd dɪˈsɪʒən/

Nouns

assumption /əˈsʌmʃən/
audition /ɔːˈdɪʃən/
auto focus /ˈɔːtəʊ ˈfəʊkəs/
claim /kleɪm/
clip /klɪp/
coastguard /ˈkəʊsgaːd/
emergency services /ɪˈmɜːdʒənsi ˈsɜːvɪsɪz/
link /lɪŋk/
opening /ˈəʊpənɪŋ/
pier /pɪə/
prejudice /ˈpredʒʊdɪs/
screen /skriːn/
staff /staːf/
superior /suːˈpɪəriə/
tide /taɪd/
venue /ˈvenjuː/

Verbs

demote /dɪˈməʊt/
impart /ɪmˈpaːt/
negate /nɪˈgeɪt/
overhear /ˌəʊvəˈhɪə/
paddle /ˈpædl/
pass with flying colours /paːs wɪð ˈflaɪɪŋ ˈkʌləz/
reinstate /ˌriːɪnˈsteɪt/
shatter /ˈʃætə/

Adjectives

humiliating /hjuːˈmɪlieɪtɪŋ/
loyal /ˈlɔɪəl/
needless /ˈniːdləs/
probationary /prʊˈbeɪʃənəri/
unable /ʌnˈeɪbl/
unbiased /ʌnˈbaɪəst/
unhelpful /ʌnˈhelpfəl/

Speaking

a bit of a long story /ə bɪt əv ə lɒŋ ˈstɔːri/
I think I'd have to say … /aɪ θɪŋk aɪd hæv tə seɪ/
let me think a moment. /let miː θɪŋk ə ˈməʊmənt/
perhaps you could tell us … /pəˈhæps juː kʊd tel ʌs/
Sure, fire away. /ʃɔː faɪə əˈweɪ/
tell us a bit about yourself … /tel ʌs ə bɪt əˈbaʊt jɔːˈself/
would you mind if I asked you … /wʊd jə maɪnd ɪf aɪ aːskt juː/

Unit 3

Advertising

commercial (n) /kəˈmɜːʃəl/
hoarding (n) /ˈhɔːdɪŋ/
jingle (n) /ˈdʒɪŋgl/
logo (n) /ˈləʊgəʊ/
sandwich board (n) /ˈsænwɪdʒ bɔːd/
slogan (n) /ˈsləʊgən/

Nouns

activist /ˈæktɪvɪst/
band-aid solution /ˈbænd eɪd səˈluːʃən/
binge /bɪndʒ/
core ingredient /kɔː ɪnˈgriːdiənt/
global warming /ˌgləʊbəl ˈwɔːmɪŋ/
hybrid car /ˈhaɪbrɪd kaː/
industrial emissions /ɪnˈdʌstriəl ɪˈmɪʃənz/
plunge /plʌndʒ/
pop-up /ˈpɒpʌp/
responsibility /rɪˌspɒnsɪˈbɪlɪti/
retail calendar /ˈriːteɪl ˈkælɪndə/
shift /ʃɪft/
target audience /ˈtaːgɪt ˈɔːdiəns/

Verbs

back (something) up /bæk ʌp/
be on to a winner /biː ɒn tuː ə ˈwɪnə/
cut (something) up /ˈkʌt ʌp/
entice /ɪnˈtaɪs/
figure (something) out /ˈfɪgə aʊt/
fit in /fɪt ɪn/
go for (something) /gəʊ fɔː/
justify /ˈdʒʌstɪfaɪ/
outline /ˈaʊtlaɪn/
provoke /prəˈvəʊk/
shed light on (something) /ʃed laɪt ɒn/
thrive /θraɪv/

Adjectives

affluent /ˈæfluənt/
ecological /ˌiːkəˈlɒdʒɪkəl/
ethical /ˈeθɪkəl/
frantic /ˈfræntɪk/
interchangeable /ˌɪntəˈtʃeɪndʒəbl/

non-commercial /ˌnɒn
    kəˈmɜːʃəl/
profound /prəˈfaʊnd/
solid /ˈsɒlɪd/
useless /ˈjuːsləs/

Adverbs

desperately /ˈdespərətli/
fundamentally
    /ˌfʌndəˈmentəli/
incredibly /ɪnˈkredɪbli/
politically /pəˈlɪtɪkli/
proudly /ˈpraʊdli/
surprisingly /səˈpraɪzɪŋli/
virtually /ˈvɜːtjuəli/

Unit 4

Feeling stressed

be too hard on yourself /biː
    tuː ˈhɑːd ɒn jɔːˈself/
chill out /tʃɪl aʊt/
let things get on top of you
    /let θɪŋz get ɒn ˈtɒp ɒv
    juː/
overdo it /ˌəʊvəˈduː ɪt/
put (your) feet up /pʊt ˈfiːt
    ʌp/
take a deep breath /teɪk eɪ
    ˈdiːp breθ/
take some exercise /teɪk sʌm
    ˈeksəsaɪz/
your blood pressure soars /jə
    blʌd ˈpreʃə sɔːz/
your forehead starts pouring
    with sweat /jə ˈfɔːhed
    stɑːts ˈpɔːrɪŋ wɪð swet/
your hands feel clammy and
    cold /jə hændz fiːl
    ˈklæmi ænd kəʊld/
your head feels like it's going to
    explode /jə hed fiːlz laɪk
    ɪts ˈgəʊɪŋ tuː ɪkˈspləʊd/
your heart starts pounding
    /jə hɑːt stɑːts ˈpaʊndɪŋ/
your mind starts racing /jə
    maɪnd stɑːts ˈreɪsɪŋ/
your mouth dries up /jə
    maʊθ draɪz ʌp/

Nouns

anxiety /æŋˈzaɪəti/
deadline /ˈdedlaɪn/
depression /dɪˈpreʃən/
insomnia /ɪnˈsɒmniə/
investigation
    /ɪnˌvestɪˈgeɪʃən/
panic attack /ˈpænɪk əˈtæk/
pressure /ˈpreʃə/
principal /ˈprɪnsɪpl/
self-esteem /ˌselfɪˈstiːm/
stress buster /stres ˈbʌstə/
symptom /ˈsɪmtəm/
tiredness /ˈtaɪədnəs/

Verbs

aggravate /ˈægrəveɪt/
assess /əˈses/
gulp down /gʌlp ˈdaʊn/
haunt /hɔːnt/
implement /ˈɪmplɪment/
pick on (someone) /pɪk ˈɒn/
recommend /ˌrekəˈmend/
relieve /rɪˈliːv/
summon /ˈsʌmən/
tackle /ˈtækl/
usher /ˈʌʃə/

Adjectives

counterproductive
    /ˌkaʊntəprəˈdʌktɪv/
dreaded /ˈdredɪd/
endangered /ɪnˈdeɪndʒəd/
excess /ekˈses/
full-blown /ˌfʊlˈbləʊn/
hyper-vigilant /ˈhaɪpə
    ˈvɪdʒɪlənt/
invaluable /ɪnˈvæljʊbl/
paranoid /ˈpærənɔɪd/

Adverbs

essentially /ɪˈsentʃəli/
excessively /ekˈsesɪvli/
inevitably /ɪˈnevɪtəbli/
productively /prəˈdʌktɪvli/

Unit 5

Crime

bogus (adj) /ˈbəʊgəs/
con (someone) out of (v) /kɒn
    ˈaʊt ɒv/
confess (v) /kənˈfes/
conman (n) /ˈkɒnmæn/
deception (n) /dɪˈsepʃən/
defraud (v) /dɪˈfrɔːd/
deny (v) /dɪˈnaɪ/
embezzlement (n)
    /ɪmˈbezlmənt/
fake (adj) /feɪk/
forge (v) /fɔːdʒ/
give (someone) the slip (v)
    /gɪv ðə slɪp/
identity theft (n) /aɪˈdentɪti
    θeft/
mislead (v) /ˌmɪsˈliːd/
outsmart (v) /ˌaʊtˈsmɑːt/
scam (n) /skæm/
white-collar crime (n) /ˌwaɪt
    ˈkɒlə kraɪm/

War and peace

battle (n) /ˈbætl/
casualty (n) /ˈkæʒjuəlti/
declare war on (v) /dɪˈkleə
    wɔː ɒn/
espionage (n) /ˈespiənɑːʒ/

intelligence officer (n)
    /ɪnˈtelɪdʒəns ˈɒfɪsə/
interrogation (n)
    /ɪnˌterəˈgeɪʃən/
invade (v) /ɪnˈveɪd/
pass (yourself) off as (v) /pɑːs
    ɒf əz/
peace negotiation (n) /piːs
    nɪˌgəʊʃiˈeɪʃən/
peace treaty (n) /piːs ˈtriːti/
recruit (v) /rɪˈkruːt/
resistance (adj) /rɪˈzɪstəns/
Resistance (n) /rɪˈzɪstəns/
secret agent (n) /ˈsiːkrət
    ˈeɪdʒənt/
sign (v) /saɪn/
spy (n) /spaɪ/
surrender (v) /sərˈendə/

Nouns

admission /ədˈmɪʃən/
assiduity /ˌæsɪˈdjuːɪti/
background /ˈbækgraʊnd/
columnist /ˈkɒləmnɪst/
contestant /kənˈtestənt/
cover story /ˈkʌvə ˌstɔːri/
deputy editor /ˈdepjuti
    ˈedɪtə/
network /ˈnetwɜːk/
retirement fund /rɪˈtaɪəmənt
    fʌnd/
savings /ˈseɪvɪŋz/
sense of duty /sens əv
    ˈdjuːti/
smirk /smɜːk/
stockbroker /ˈstɒkˌbrəʊkə/
thrill /θrɪl/
tribal chief /ˈtraɪbəl tʃiːf/

Verbs

cause harm to (someone)
    /kɔːz ˈhɑːm tə/
cheat (someone) out of /tʃiːt
    aʊt ɒv/
combat /ˈkɒmbæt/
deposit /dɪˈpɒzɪt/
disclose /dɪsˈkləʊz/
embark /ɪmˈbɑːk/
prevail /prɪˈveɪl/

Adjectives

audacious /ɔːˈdeɪʃəs/
dreadful /ˈdredfəl/
grave /greɪv/
harrowing /ˈhærəʊɪŋ/
irresponsible /ˌɪrɪˈspɒnsɪbl/
patriotic /ˌpætriˈɒtɪk/
prudent /ˈpruːdənt/
witty /ˈwɪti/

Adverbs

assuredly /əˈʃɔːɪdli/
ironically /aɪəˈrɒnɪkli/
utterly /ˈʌtəli/

Unit 6

Expressions with story

a likely story /ə ˈlaɪkli ˈstɔːri/
a sob story /ə sɒb ˈstɔːri/
end of story /end əv ˈstɔːri/
make up a story /meɪk ʌp ə
    ˈstɔːri/
(someone's) side of the story
    /saɪd əv ðə ˈstɔːri/
the same old story /ðə seɪm
    əʊld ˈstɔːri/
the story of my life /ðə ˈstɔːri
    əv maɪ laɪf/
to cut a long story short /tə
    kʌt ə lɒŋ ˈstɔːri ʃɔːt/

Nouns

antidote /ˈæntɪdəʊt/
compulsion /kəmˈpʌlʃən/
contamination
    /kənˌtæmɪˈneɪʃən/
cyberspace /ˈsaɪbəspeɪs/
essay /ˈeseɪ/
hairdo /ˈheəduː/
implication /ˌɪmplɪˈkeɪʃən/
myth /mɪθ/
roommate /ˈruːmmeɪt/
tutor /ˈtjuːtə/
urban legend /ˈɜːbən
    ˈledʒənd/
venom /ˈvenəm/

Verbs

come across (something) /kʌm
    əˈkrɒs/
crop up /krɒp ˈʌp/
curse /kɜːs/
diagnose /ˈdaɪəgnəʊz/
fill (somebody) in /fɪl ˈɪn/
hold a conference/meeting
    /həʊld ə ˈkɒnfərəns
    ˈmiːtɪŋ/
itch /ɪtʃ/
lead to /liːd tuː/
let (something) down /let
    ˈdaʊn/
trace back to /treɪs bæk tuː/

Adjectives

broke /brəʊk/
horrific /həˈrɪfɪk/
integral /ˈɪntɪgrəl/
irrelevant /ɪˈreləvənt/

Adverbs

by word of mouth /baɪ wɜːd
    əv maʊθ/
entirely /ɪnˈtaɪəli/
unexpectedly
    /ˌʌnɪkˈspektɪdli/

Speaking

again and again and again /əˈgen ænd əˈgen ænd əˈgen/

all of a sudden /ɔːl əv ə ˈsʌdən/

anything and everything /ˈeniθɪŋ ænd ˈevriθɪŋ/

kind of /kaɪnd ɒv/

off we went /ɒf wiː went/

the amazing thing /ðiː əˈmeɪzɪŋ θɪŋ/

too good to be true /tuː gʊd tə biː truː/

would you believe it /wʊd jə bɪˈliːv ɪt/

Unit 7

Metaphors to describe emotions

be on top of the world /biː ɒn tɒp əv ðə wɜːld/

be really cut up /biː ˈrɪəli kʌt ʌp/

(don't) know where to put yourself /nəʊ weə tə put jɔːˈself/

feel a bit down in the dumps /fiːl ə bɪt daʊn ɪn ðə dʌmps/

feel like you're banging (your) head against a brick wall /fiːl laɪk jɔː ˈbæŋɪŋ jə hed əˈgenst ə brɪk wɔːl/

have a screw loose /hæv ə skruː luːs/

have butterflies in (your) stomach /hæv ˈbʌtəflaɪz ɪn ˈstʌmək/

keep (your) hair on /kiːp heə ɒn/

(something) makes (your) blood boil /meɪks blʌd bɔɪl/

Nouns

apprenticeship /əˈprentɪsʃɪp/

arson /ˈɑːsən/

atrium /ˈeɪtriəm/

campaigner /ˌkæmˈpeɪnə/

council /ˈkaʊnsəl/

helipad /ˈhelɪpæd/

intellect /ˈɪntəlekt/

light-heartedness /ˌlaɪtˈhɑːtɪdnəs/

lobby /ˈlɒbi/

metaphor /ˈmetəfɔː/

racism /ˈreɪsɪzəm/

Verbs

appal /əˈpɔːl/

be into (something) /biː ˈɪntə/

come out /kʌm ˈaʊt/

derive /dɪˈraɪv/

go on /gəʊ ˈɒn/

juggle /ˈdʒʌgl/

put (something) out /pʊt ˈaʊt/

refer to /rɪˈfɜː tuː/

resemble /rɪˈzembl/

revive /rɪˈvaɪv/

set on fire /set ɒn faɪə/

spur on /spɜː ˈɒn/

Adjectives

bulbous /ˈbʌlbəs/

curving /ˈkɜːvɪŋ/

embarrassed /ɪmˈbærəst/

fertile /ˈfɜːtaɪl/

frustrated /frʌsˈtreɪtɪd/

grateful /ˈgreɪtfəl/

irregular /ɪˈregjələ/

misshapen /mɪsˈʃeɪpən/

remarkable /rɪˈmɑːkəbl/

swollen /ˈswəʊlən/

synonymous /sɪˈnɒnɪməs/

trivial /ˈtrɪviəl/

vibrant /ˈvaɪbrənt/

vivid /ˈvɪvɪd/

Adverbs

deliberately /dɪˈlɪbərətli/

horribly /ˈhɒrəbli/

largely /ˈlɑːdʒli/

occasionally /əˈkeɪʒənəli/

originally /əˈrɪdʒənəli/

politically /pəˈlɪtɪkli/

variously /ˈveəriəsli/

virtually /ˈvɜːtjuəli/

Unit 8

Money

cash card (n) /ˈkæʃ ˌkɑːd/

currency (n) /ˈkʌrənsi/

earn a living (v) /ɜːn ə ˈlɪvɪŋ/

economic (adj) /ˌiːkəˈnɒmɪk/

economy (n) /ɪˈkɒnəmi/

interest rate (n) /ˈɪntrəst reɪt/

make money (v) /meɪk ˈmʌni/

open an account (v) /ˈəʊpən æn əˈkaʊnt/

purchase (v) /ˈpɜːtʃəs/

take out a loan (v) /teɪk aʊt ə ləʊn/

Informal expressions

a piece of cake /ə piːs əv keɪk/

dash off /ˈdæʃ ɒf/

get the green light /get ðə griːn laɪt/

grab a bite /græb ə baɪt/

just kidding /dʒʌst ˈkɪdɪŋ/

kids /kɪdz/

Nouns

approval /əˈpruːvəl/

asteroid space resort /ˈæstərɔɪd ˈspeɪs rɪˈzɔːt/

boffin /ˈbɒfɪn/

brainchild /ˈbreɪntʃaɪld/

chat room /ˈtʃæt ˌruːm/

cyber junky /ˈsaɪbə ˈdʒʌnki/

headset /ˈhedset/

memory transplant service /ˈmeməri trænˈsplɑːnt ˈsɜːvɪs/

option /ˈɒpʃən/

supplier /səˈplaɪə/

Verbs

colonise /ˈkɒlənaɪz/

end up /end ʌp/

hatch /hætʃ/

implant /ɪmˈplɑːnt/

join up /dʒɔɪn ʌp/

live out /lɪv ˈaʊt/

manufacture /ˌmænjʊˈfækʃə/

recall /rɪˈkɔːl/

Adjectives

bearable /ˈbeərəbl/

distant /ˈdɪstənt/

earthbound /ˈɜːθbaʊnd/

fancy /ˈfænsi/

ferocious /fəˈrəʊʃəs/

infinite /ˈɪnfɪnət/

multi-sensory /ˈmʌltiˌsensəri/

promotional /prəˈməʊʃənəl/

sinister /ˈsɪnɪstə/

three-dimensional /ˌθriːdɪˈmenʃənəl/

trustworthy /ˈtrʌstˌwɜːði/

Adverbs

actually /ˈæktʃuəli/

especially /ɪˈspeʃəli/

overwhelmingly /ˌəʊvəˈwelmɪŋli/

Unit 9

Habits and gestures

bite (your) nails /baɪt neɪlz/

blink /blɪŋk/

cough /kɒf/

fiddle with (your) hair /ˈfɪdl wɪð heə/

fold (your) hands behind (your) head /fəʊld hændz bɪˈhaɪnd hed/

rub (your) forehead/hands together /rʌb ˈfɔːhed/ hændz təˈgeðə/

stroke (your) chin /strəʊk tʃɪn/

tilt (your) head /tɪlt hed/

Nouns

anguish /ˈæŋgwɪʃ/

ban /bæn/

bow /baʊ/

cargo ship /ˈkɑːgəʊ ʃɪp/

driving force /ˈdraɪvɪŋ fɔːs/

flare /fleə/

fortification /ˌfɔːtɪfɪˈkeɪʃən/

gaze /geɪz/

heart transplant /hɑːt trænˈsplɑːnt/

might /maɪt/

mirror neuron /ˈmɪrə ˈnjʊərɒn/

mirroring /ˈmɪrərɪŋ/

moat /məʊt/

neuroscience /ˌnjʊərəʊˈsaɪəns/

petrol tanker /ˈpetrəl ˈtæŋkə/

propeller /prəˈpelə/

rapport /ræˈpɔː/

scenario /sɪˈnɑːriəʊ/

sentinel /ˈsentɪnəl/

social disorder /ˈsəʊʃəl dɪˈsɔːdə/

speck /spek/

urge /ɜːdʒ/

veto /ˈviːtəʊ/

wake /weɪk/

wreck /rek/

Verbs

chop /tʃɒp/

churn /tʃɜːn/

crouch /kraʊtʃ/

empathise /ˈempəθaɪz/

girdle /ˈgɜːdl/

imitate /ˈɪmɪteɪt/

incorporate /ɪnˈkɔːpəreɪt/

languish /ˈlæŋgwɪʃ/

reap /riːp/

refute /rɪˈfjuːt/

replicate /ˈreplɪkeɪt/

ricochet /ˈrɪkəʃeɪ/

slide /slaɪd/

snore /snɔː/

surge /sɜːdʒ/

trudge /trʌdʒ/

undergo /ˌʌndəˈgəʊ/

Adjectives

awesome /ˈɔːsəm/

behavioural /bɪˈheɪvjərəl/

controversial /ˌkɒntrəˈvɜːʃəl/

cranky /ˈkræŋki/

frothy /ˈfrɒθi/

imitative /ˈɪmɪtətɪv/

languishing /ˈlæŋgwɪʃɪŋ/

looming /ˈluːmɪŋ/

momentous /məˈmentəs/

pointless /ˈpɔɪntləs/

revealing /rɪˈviːlɪŋ/

staunch /stɔːnʃ/

stunning /ˈstʌnɪŋ/

subtle /'sʌtl/
tragic /'trædʒɪk/
unfettered /ʌn'fetəd/
vast /vɑːst/

Adverbs

genetically /dʒə'netɪkli/
relentlessly /rɪ'lentləsli/
undeniably /ˌʌndɪ'naɪəbli/
undoubtedly /ʌn'daʊtɪdli/
unquestionably
    /ʌn'kwestʃənəbli/
utterly /'ʌtəli/

Unit 10

Success and failure

blow it (v) /bləʊ ɪt/
fall through (v) /fɔːl θruː/
fulfil (v) /fʊl'fɪl/
go wrong (v) /gəʊ rɒŋ/
make it (v) /meɪk ɪt/
mess (something) up (v) /mes
    ʌp/
overcome (v) /ˌəʊvə'kʌm/
pull (something) off (v) /pʊl
    ɒf/

Nouns

backlash /'bæklæʃ/
belongings /bɪ'lɒŋɪŋz/
community service
    /kə'mjuːnəti 'sɜːvɪs/
feat /fiːt/
finishing line /'fɪnɪʃɪŋ laɪn/
hesitation /ˌhezɪ'teɪʃən/
insult /'ɪnsʌlt/
mid-race collapse /mɪd reɪs
    kə'læps/
opponent /ə'pəʊnənt/
paralysis /pə'ræləsɪs/
penalty /'penəlti/
spectator sport /spek'teɪtə
    spɔːt/
standing ovation /'stændɪŋ
    ə'veɪʃən/
suspension /sə'spenʃən/

Verbs

award /ə'wɔːd/
butt /bʌt/
collapse /kə'læps/
criticise /'krɪtɪsaɪz/
fulfil (your) ambition /fʊl'fɪl
    æm'bɪʃən/
lambast /læm'bæst/
seal /siːl/
size up /saɪz ʌp/
slump /slʌmp/
smash /smæʃ/
stagger /'stægə/
tread /tred/

Adjectives

acceptable /ək'septəbəl/
gruelling /'gruːlɪŋ/
illegal /ɪ'liːgəl/
inappropriate
    /ˌɪnə'prəʊpriət/
inevitable /ɪ'nevɪtəbl/

Adverbs

bitterly /'bɪtəli/
comparatively
    /kəm'pærətɪvli/
coolly /'kuːlli/
eventually /ɪ'ventjuəli/
magnificently
    /mæg'nɪfɪsəntli/
partially /'pɑːʃəli/

Speaking

anyway, … /'eniweɪ/
as it happens, … /æz ɪt
    'hæpənz/
by the way, … /baɪ ðə weɪ/
Can you just bear with me for a
    moment? /kæn juː dʒʌst
    beə wɪð miː fər ə
    'məʊmənt/
few and far between /fjuː
    ænd fɑː bɪ'twiːn/
in fact, … /ɪn fækt/
just as a matter of interest, …
    /dʒʌst æzə 'mætə əv
    'ɪntrəst/
now, the first thing I want to
    say … /naʊ ðə 'fɜːst θɪŋ
    aɪ wɒnt tə seɪ/
right - going back to … /raɪt
    'gəʊɪŋ bæk tuː/

Unit 11

From human to hero

pant (v) /pænt/
puny (adj) /'pjuːni/
short-sighted (adj) /ˌʃɔːt
    'saɪtɪd/
slouched (adj) /slaʊtʃt/
speed of light (n) /spiːd əv
    laɪt/
squint (v) /skwɪnt/
strength (n) /streŋθ/
superhuman (adj)
    /ˌsuːpə'hjuːmən/
X-ray vision (n) /'eks reɪ
    'vɪʒən/

Nouns

arch-enemy /ɑːtʃ 'enəmi/
breath /breθ/
conception /kən'sepʃən/
conspiracy /kən'spɪrəsi/
credits /'kredɪts/
cultural gap /'kʌltʃərəl gæp/

descendent /dɪ'sendənt/
encounter /ɪn'kaʊntə/
foe /fəʊ/
frailty /'freɪlti/
incarnation /ˌɪnkɑː'neɪʃən/
make-believe /'meɪkbɪˌliːv/
mastermind /'mɑːstəmaɪnd/
mutant /'mjuːtənt/
public relations officer
    /'pʌblɪk rɪ'leɪʃənz 'ɒfɪsə/
sequel /'siːkwəl/
solitude /'sɒlɪtjuːd/
sorcery /'sɔːsəri/
twist /twɪst/
warrior /'wɒriə/

Verbs

be short of (something) /bi
    ʃɔːt ɒv/
design /dɪ'zaɪn/
eliminate /ɪ'lɪmɪneɪt/
launch /lɔːnʃ/
patrol /pə'trəʊl/
reach a conclusion /riːtʃ ə
    kən'kluːʒən/
power /paʊə/

Adjectives

crucial /'kruːʃəl/
fictitious /fɪk'tɪʃəs/
handy /'hændi/
hardcore /'hɑːdkɔː/
life-threatening
    /'laɪf ˌθretənɪŋ/
medieval /ˌmedi'iːvəl/
microscopic
    /ˌmaɪkrə'skɒpɪk/
phenomenal /fə'nɒmɪnəl/
poisonous /'pɔɪzənəs/
supernatural
    /ˌsuːpə'nætʃərəl/
unassuming /ˌʌnə'sjuːmɪŋ/
unwatchable /ˌʌn'wɒʃəbl/

Adverbs

directly /dɪ'rekli/
swiftly /'swɪftli/
ultimately /'ʌltɪmətli/

Unit 12

Expressions with time

at all times /æt ɔːl taɪmz/
fill (your) time /fɪl taɪm/
give (someone) time /gɪv
    taɪm/
have time on (your) hands
    /hæv taɪm ɒn hændz/
in no time at all /ɪn nəʊ taɪm
    æt ɔːl/
kill time /kɪl taɪm/
make time /meɪk taɪm/
time's up /taɪmz ʌp/

Nouns

barometer /bə'rɒmɪtə/
castaway /'kɑːstəweɪ/
dilemma /dɪ'lemə/
hummingbird /'hʌmɪŋbɜːd/
life plan /laɪf plæn/
patch /pætʃ/
peninsulas /pə'nɪnsjʊləz/
ranger /'reɪndʒə/
set-up /set ʌp/
sustenance /'sʌstɪnəns/
wind generator /wɪnd
    'dʒenəreɪtə/

Verbs

be in charge of /bi ɪn tʃɑːdʒ
    ɒv/
drop by /drɒp baɪ/
get into (something) /get
    'ɪntə/
hum /hʌm/
tear down (something) /teə
    daʊn/
wander /'wɒndə/

Adjectives

ambiguous /æm'bɪgjuəs/
catchy /'kætʃi/
dense /dents/
fruitless /'fruːtləs/
idle /'aɪdl/
land-bound /lænd baʊnd/
recreational /ˌrekri'eɪʃənəl/
remote /rɪ'məʊt/
repetitive /rɪ'petətɪv/
undisturbed /ˌʌndɪ'stɜːbd/

Unit 13

Verbs referring to the future

be about to /bi ə'baʊt tuː/
be bound to /bi 'baʊnd tuː/
be due to /bi 'djuː tuː/
be off to /bi 'ɒf tuː/
be supposed to /bi sə'pəʊzd
    tuː/
be thinking of /bi 'θɪŋkɪŋ
    ɒv/

Life choices

change careers /tʃeɪndʒ
    kə'rɪəz/
drop out of college/university
    /drɒp 'aʊt ɒv 'kɒlɪdʒ
    ˌjuːnɪ'vɜːsɪti/
leave school /liːv 'skuːl/
pay off/take out student loans
    /peɪ ɒf/teɪk aʊt
    ˌstjuːdənt 'ləʊnz/
settle down /'setl daʊn/
start a family /stɑːt ə
    'fæməli/

take a year off /teɪk ə jɪə ɒf/
take early retirement /teɪk ˈɜːli rɪˈtaɪəmənt/

Nouns

activist /ˈæktɪvɪst/
exhaust fumes /ɪgˈzɔːst fjuːmz/
funding /ˈfʌndɪŋ/
nuclear weapon /ˈnjuːkliə ˈwepən/
scent /sent/

Verbs

browse /braʊz/
daydream /ˈdeɪdriːm/
retire /rɪˈtaɪə/
soothe /suːð/

Adjectives

fragrant /ˈfreɪgrənt/
grotty /ˈgrɒti/
leafy /ˈliːfi/
prohibitive /prəˈhɪbɪtɪv/
ripe /raɪp/
soothing /ˈsuːðɪŋ/
suburban /səˈbɜːbən/
undaunted /ʌnˈdɔːntɪd/
unsoured /ʌnˈsaʊəd/
wrinkled /ˈrɪŋkld/

Unit 14

Commonly confused words

advice (n) /ədˈvaɪs/
advise (v) /ədˈvaɪz/
affects (v) /əˈfekts/
effects (n) /ɪˈfekts/
ensure (v) /ɪnˈʃɔː/
insure (v) /ɪnˈʃɔː/
lay (v) /leɪ/
lie (v / n) /laɪ/
loose (adj) /luːs/
lose (v) /luːz/
persecute (v) /ˈpɜːsɪkjuːt/
prosecute (v) /ˈprɒsɪkjuːt/
raised (v) /reɪzd/
risen (adj) /ˈrɪzən/
sensible (adj) /ˈsensɪbl/
sensitive (adj) /ˈsensɪtɪv/

Nouns

biogerentology /baɪədʒərentˈɒlədʒi/
consultation /ˌkɒnsʌlˈteɪʃən/
diversity /daɪˈvɜːsɪti/
extension /ɪkˈstenʃən/
facelift /ˈfeɪslɪft/
manipulation /məˌnɪpjʊˈleɪʃən/
medication /ˌmedɪˈkeɪʃən/
method /ˈmeθəd/

nose job /nəʊz dʒɒb/
nutrient /ˈnjuːtriənt/
pharmaceuticals /ˌfɑːməˈsuːtɪkəlz/
plastic surgery /ˌplæstɪk ˈsɜːdʒəri/
self-confidence /ˌself ˈkɒnfɪdəns/
shoplifter /ˈʃɒpˌlɪftə/
vanity /ˈvænɪti/
wrinkle /ˈrɪŋkl/

Verbs

bombard /ˈbɒmbɑːd/
cooperate /kəʊˈɒpəreɪt/
enhance /ɪnˈhɑːns/
insure /ɪnˈʃɔː/
tease /tiːz/

Adjectives

accessible /əkˈsesəbl/
acute /əˈkjuːt/
aesthetic /esˈθetɪk/
assertive /əˈsɜːtɪv/
biochemical /ˌbaɪəˈkemɪkəl/
grotesque /grəˈtesk/
immaculate /ɪˈmækjʊlət/
mortal /ˈmɔːtəl/
overwhelming /ˌəʊvəˈwelmɪŋ/
prolonging /prəˈlɒŋɪŋ/
unscrupulous /ʌnˈskruːpjʊləs/

Speaking

Exactly. /ɪgˈzækli/
I mean, ... /aɪ miːn/
I'd have thought ... /aɪd əv θɔːt/
(I really don't agree,) though. /ðəʊ/
on the other hand, ... /ɒn ðiː ˈʌðə hænd/
tell you what, ... /tel juː wɒt/
the thing is, ... /ðə θɪŋ ɪz/
to be honest, ... /tə biː ˈɒnɪst/
to tell you the truth, ... /tə tel juː ðə truːθ/
we're going round in circles /wɪə ˈgəʊɪŋ raʊnd ɪn ˈsɜːklz/

Unit 15

Old and new

contemporary (adj) /kənˈtempərəri/
novel (adj) /ˈnɒvəl/
obsolete (adj) /ˌɒbsəˈliːt/
old-fashioned (adj) /ˌəʊldˈfæʃənd/
outdated (adj) /ˌaʊtˈdeɪtɪd/

out-of-date (adj) /ˌaʊtəvˈdeɪt/
up-to-date (adj) /ˌʌptəˈdeɪt/

Nouns

artefact /ˈɑːtɪfækt/
art gallery /ɑːt ˈgæləri/
assortment /əˈsɔːtmənt/
consent /kənˈsent/
cotton mill /ˈkɒtən mɪl/
craftsmanship /ˈkrɑːftsmənʃɪp/
footwear /ˈfʊtweə/
four-storey building /fɔː ˈstɔːri ˈbɪldɪŋ/
gem /dʒem/
lawnmower /ˈlɔːnˌməʊə/
maintenance /ˈmeɪntɪnəns/
national sporting event /ˈnæʃənəl ˈspɔːtɪŋ ɪˈvent/
nomination /ˌnɒmɪˈneɪʃən/
obsession /əbˈseʃən/
preservation /ˌprezəˈveɪʃən/
psychiatry /saɪˈkaɪətri/
puppy /ˈpʌpi/
shrink /ʃrɪŋk/
theme park /ˈθiːm ˌpɑːk/

Verbs

be on display /biː ɒn dɪˈspleɪ/
boast /bəʊst/
renew /rɪˈnjuː/
renovate /ˈrenəveɪt/
restore /rɪˈstɔː/
safeguard /ˈseɪfgɑːd/
update /ˈʌpdeɪt/

Adjectives

countless /ˈkaʊntləs/
eventual /ɪˈventjuəl/
everlasting /ˌevəˈlɑːstɪŋ/
extraordinary /ɪkˈstrɔːdɪnəri/
fluorescent /fluəˈresənt/
genuine /ˈdʒenjuɪn/
gloomy /ˈgluːmi/
invaluable /ɪnˈvæljʊbl/
legendary /ˈledʒəndri/
misspent /mɪsˈspent/
psychedelic /ˌsaɪkəˈdelɪk/
unappreciated /ˌʌnəˈpriːʃieɪtɪd/

Adverbs

actively /ˈæktɪvli/
arguably /ˈɑːgjuəbli/
barely /ˈbeəli/
democratically /ˌdeməˈkrætɪkli/
quintessentially /ˌkwɪntɪˈsenʃəli/
solely /ˈsəʊlli/

Unit 16

Teenspeak

biter (n) /ˈbaɪtə/
busted (adj) /ˈbʌstɪd/
da bomb (n) /ˌdæˈbɒm/
dorky (adj) /ˈdɔːki/
slacker (n) /ˈslækə/
the 411 (n) /ðiː ˈfɔːwʌnwʌn/
totally (adv) /ˈtəʊtəli/
whatever (adv) /wɒtˈevə/

Nouns

curry /ˈkʌri/
high culture /haɪ ˈkʌltʃə/
showmanship /ˈʃəʊmənʃɪp/
stage works /steɪdʒ wɜːks/
time capsule /ˈtaɪm ˌkæpsjuːl/
transition /trænˈzɪʃən/
vitality /vaɪˈtælɪti/

Verbs

choreograph /ˈkɒriəgrɑːf/
disdain /dɪsˈdeɪn/
exploit /ˈɪksplɔɪt/
flow in /fləʊ ɪn/
hesitate /ˈhezɪteɪt/

Adjectives

balletic /bæˈletɪk/
intense /ɪnˈtens/
open-minded /ˌəʊpənˈmaɪndɪd/
second-hand /ˌsekənd ˈhænd/
sneaking suspicion /ˈsniːkɪŋ səˈspɪʃən/
stuffy /ˈstʌfi/
stylised /ˈstaɪlaɪzd/

Adverbs

carefully /ˈkeəfəli/
fiercely /ˈfɪəsli/
incredibly /ɪnˈkredɪbli/
occasionally /əˈkeɪʒənəli/